you
can make
a difference

God bless you!
Ruth Youngdahl Nelson

you can make a difference

RUTH YOUNGDAHL NELSON

AUGSBURG PUBLISHING HOUSE
Minneapolis, Minnesota

Contents

To my husband Clarence
whose commitment
to the Lord
has made such a difference
in our lives!

Preface

It is an interesting exercise to search one's heart for the earliest remembrance of the awareness of God. Mine is the Christmas time when I was almost four. (My birthday is in January.) And I guess it wasn't an all-at-once experience but a gradual growing one as my mother taught me the song I was to sing at the Sunday school program.

That was a very special occasion when everybody came to hear the children perform. And afterward each one was given a box (like the animal cracker ones) of Christmas-mix candy, and a book of stories about good little boys and girls. Sometimes the handles of those boxes broke and the contents scattered in all directions. Then there would be tears.

But back to the song. Through all these ensuing years its message has been indelibly printed on my mind. And when I have been fearful, when I have felt alone, when burdens and cares have pressed in upon me, the words of the song-writer would return to bless me.

> I am Jesus' little lamb;
> Therefore glad at heart I am.
> Jesus loves me, Jesus knows me;
> All that's good and fair he shows me.
> Tends me every day the same;
> Even calls me by my name.

Even as a little child, I flavored the meaning. Since I belong to Jesus I should be glad at heart; even though he knows me (yes, the time I ate candy when it had been forbidden; the time I told a falsehood), yet he loves me. He is with me every day—and he even knows my name. I used to walk around the house, saying my own name as if he were talking to me.

I still do.

When I have had unworthy thoughts, mean ambitions, unloving judgments of others, I hear him say, "Ruth, do you want to be my follower? Do you want to have my mind?" And I have to respond quickly, "Forgive, Lord! Forgive! Help me!"

When I was six, the angel of death touched our home. We were nine then in our family. (My brother Reuben was born later.) My sister Myrtle, five years my senior, but the one next in line to me, was my guardian angel. Mother's operation for varicose veins had immobilized her for a while, and Myrtle made me her special care. She was a gold-haired lass, always thinking of others, and much older than her years.

As usual we went to school together that memorable Monday morning, playing beanbag along the way. Adams School was about ten blocks from our red-brick house on Eleventh Avenue. Everything seemed the same as any other day. But when I came out of school at noon, Hazel, our neighbor friend, came and took my hand, "You are to go home with me," she said. "Myrtle took sick and went home early."

The next morning my beloved companion and protector was gone. Her sickness was diagnosed as spinal meningitis. It was in the days before antibiotics and other amazing medicines had been discovered.

I was in a hazy maze amid all the comings and goings of people and the weeping and sorrow of my parents. With this as a backdrop, there stands out crystal clear the incident father loved to relate in the years following. It had happened at Myrtle's bedside. The Sunday night before, she had gone to church with father and the pastor's discourse had been on heaven. "Eye hath not seen, ear hath not heard what God has in store for those who love him!" Myrtle had plied Dad with questions en route home.

Now Dad was a grocery man, but he was also a Bible student and really studied the Scriptures. Our library would have done credit to any clergyman. He taught the young people's Bible class at church. So he and Myrtle had quite a conversation that evening on the way home from church. As father sat at Myrtle's bedside in the late hours of the next evening (she was burning with a temperature of 106 degrees) out of the coma in which she had been, Myrtle opened her eyes, looked at Dad, and said, "It is true, Papa; there is a paradise in heaven." Those words were to hang like a star of hope in the dark night of grief.

A few years later, Reuben was born, and he became my special charge. From the day he was born, unbeknown to his parents or anybody, his little sister prayed, "Bless Reuben and help him to grow up and be a minister when he gets big; and help me to be a missionary!"

Then came confirmation. And that was for real! Not only did my mother see that I knew my catechism backwards and forwards. She wanted me to understand what I was memorizing. How grateful I have been for all the Bible verses stored in my heart from those lessons!

Our confirmation pastor made very clear that we weren't just "graduating" from Sunday school, but that we were promising on our own to accept Christ. Values came into focus in an amazing way on confirmation Sunday by an unexpected incident. We had moved out to 40th and Lyndale and so had quite a ride to Messiah Church on 25th and Columbus. Father had left mother Augustana, the Swedish congregation, to become a charter member of the daughter, English-speaking Messiah for the sake of the children. He thought it all-important for the children to worship in the language they used daily. In those days also, girls had long hair. But mostly it was braided and tied with gay hair ribbons. It was a warm day, and our car top was down. We just didn't snap on the fussy ising-glass curtains except when it was raining! It wasn't until we reached church that I discovered my hair-ribbon was gone. And I wept! I would be different from all the other girls in our class! Then I remembered Dr. Samuel Miller, our pastor, putting his hand on my shoulder and saying, "Ruth, man looks to the outward appearance, but the Lord looks to the heart!" And guess what! Our good friend, Mrs. Gillquist, remembered that the girl living next door to her had been confirmed the previous Sunday in a neighboring church and that she had worn a white hair ribbon. So down the street she went and just before we processed in as a class, she had it on my pigtail.

How I wish I could repeat the experience of my first communion! The Holy Spirit was truly there in the believing heart of the thirteen-year-old who knelt at the altar to know the joy of God's forgiving love. But each experience of our lives is an entity in itself. Things never repeat themselves—exactly!

I sailed through the high school and college years, graduating from Minnesota College (our church academy) at sixteen. I was really still a young girl when I entered Gustavus Adolphus College that fall. It wasn't hard to fall into the fun of dormitory living on a campus where the enrollment was small enough so you could know almost everybody. And you couldn't miss the impact of that church-related school. Daily we received spiritual nourishment in chapel and in our Christianity courses. Both were compulsory. We were challenged and inspired by our professors.

On this campus, after hearing a doctor from India tell of his work, I decided that's where I wanted to go. But I was too young when I graduated, so I started teaching school, first in Miller, South Dakota, and then at Roosevelt High School in Minneapolis. Meanwhile I was corresponding with the Mission Board and the late Dr. Markley of India.

Things were coming into focus for my future plans to go to India when I attended a youth retreat at Lake Independence. Some of us who loved swimming decided to try to swim the three miles across the lake (with a rowboat accompanying us, of course). Our boat had to wait because the other swimmer had a committee meeting first. He was state president of the youth league. I chafed, but the youth manning the oars wouldn't budge. Hadn't he promised Pastor Nelson to wait? I guess I really ought to thank him, because if we hadn't waited, I might never have known the joy of "swimming" through life with a great partner! Clarence was the one. It was against rules for a young man and a young woman to be in a rowboat together in their swimming suits (and you should have seen the suits!) I wanted to swim back again, but Clarence thought it was just too much so we had no other alternative but to break the rules.

Well, that episode started the process of my being persuaded that the Lord could use me in "home" missions to which I capitulated. And August 25th, on my parents' 40th wedding anniversary that next summer, saw a dreamy-eyed school teacher float down the aisle in Messiah Church to say "I do!"

What great years we have had together! O there have been plenty of tough times. We were married during the "great" depression. And not only economically, but emotionally there were tough times when one stubborn Swede took another stubborn Swede head-on! But always there was God, the great Bringer-together, and the "I'm sorry" with its ensuing "Forgive me, beloved." More and more we grew to be a team whose goal was to serve the Christ we so deeply loved. And as our children were born each was committed to him.

Somebody asked me recently to say which I like best of all the places we have lived. First there was Minneapolis, next St. Paul, and then Duluth. From there we went to Washington, D.C., to spend the longest spate of years. And then half-way around the world to Saudi Arabia. Geneva, Switzerland was our home for three years. Then it was Chicago, and at last, come full circle, back to Minneapolis. I had to reply, "Each one at the time we lived there." How much we have learned from the people with whom we were sharing our lives! Now my husband serves at Augustana and each Sunday I sit facing the very font where my parents brought me to be baptized. Each has been a rich chapter! In Saudi Arabia 100 of our members were nurses and medical workers from India, so a part of my early dream to be a missionary to India was fulfilled! How good God can be!

In Denver, May of 1973, I was representing Minnesota in the National Convention of American Mothers. We were each given three minutes to present the story of our lives. I chose as my theme the words of the Apostle Paul, "I am a debtor!"

I'd like to reiterate them here as I remember them. I am a debtor to a loving God and Savior, Creator, and Redeemer who has put such rich meaning into my life. I am a debtor to parents who taught me and the nine others of their children that life is a stewardship, that we are born to serve and love God, by loving and serving our fellowmen; that if we permit Christ to live in us each of us can make a difference; that we are our brother's keeper, and that life will find fulfillment only as we remember this. I am a debtor to my church which nourished and inspired faith and love and taught me that a Christian must grow. I am a debtor to my country in which I could get an education, in which I'm free to worship according to my conscience, in which I'm free to criticize it, because I love it. I am a debtor to a husband who is fun to live with, whose first desire is to serve the Lord, who has helped me to grow and dream and love. I am a debtor to children who have shamed me by their dedication, whose compulsion and understanding and love are beyond anything I ever knew, who have stimulated and inspired me to press on and enlarge my plans and gifts, who have put their lives on the line again and again in serving their Lord and sharing his love with others. Our children by birth and also our foster children have enriched our lives beyond words to describe.

I am a debtor to countless friends whose love and companionship and inspiration are a constant joy and encouragement. I think of the little prayer groups in Washington, D.C., in Saudi Arabia, in Geneva, Switzerland, and now in Minneapolis. What a fellowship!

Why have I written all this? Only to witness what the Lord can do with one person! Only to witness how *you* can make a difference in a home, in an office, in school, in the community, in your country, in the world, if only you will permit the presence of Christ to so live in you as to mould your opinions, motivate your actions, spur you on to the translating of his love into human relationships!

Now Is the Best Minute of the Day

*Be most careful then, how you con-
duct yourselves: like sensible men, not
like simpletons. Use the present opportunity to the full, for these are
evil days.* EPHESIANS 5:15

*In all this, remember how critical the
moment is. It is time for you to wake
out of sleep.* ROMANS 13:11

What is your best minute of the day?

Psychologists tell us our most im-
pressionable moments are the last ones before sleep and the
first one on awakening in the morning. Most of us waste
an enormous amount of that precious commodity "time" by
either recounting the past, or living in the future. God's best
moment in your life is *now!*

As one writer said:

> I have only just a minute,
>   Only sixty seconds in it,
> Forced upon me—can't refuse it,
>   Didn't seek it, didn't choose it,
> But it's up to me to use it,
>   Give account if I abuse it;
> Just a tiny little minute
>   But eternity is in it!

Some of us may be in the position of the man in Mexi-
co. A civil engineer was building a railroad and was trying
to demonstrate how it would benefit the nation.

15

"How long," the engineer asked, "does it take you to carry your produce to market at present?"

"With a mule it takes three days," was the response.

"There you are," said the engineer. "When the new railroad is in operation, you will be able to take your produce to market and return the very same day."

"Very good, Senor," was the response. "But what will I do with the other two days?"

Michel Quoist recounts in a prayer poem "I Have Time" how through each succeeding period in our lives, our excuse is "I haven't time."

The child is too busy at play; the youth with his athletics; the student with his studies; the newly married with their home, then their children; the old folks with their doctoring, and then they have no more time.

Quoist then raises the question: "Hasn't God made a mistake in his calculations?"

And he comes up with his conclusion that God gives to each time to do what he expects each one of us to do. But he says:

> We must not lose time
> We must not waste time
> We must not kill time.

And he concludes: "I am not asking you tonight, Lord, for time to do this and then that. But your grace to do conscientiously, in the time that you give me, what you want me to do!"

The poet has said:

> Each day is a little life.

The best minute of the day is now. What God puts upon your heart to do, do!

So many things I've missed doing, Lord, because I've postponed them. Help me to use each minute in thoughts of you and in loving deeds for others. Make each minute the best, because you are in it! Amen.

What to Do with Guilt

Be gracious to me, O God, in thy true love; in the fullness of thy mercy blot out my misdeeds. Wash away all my guilt and cleanse me from sin. For well I know my misdeeds, and my sins confront me all the day long.

PSALM 51:1-3

This letter appeared in an advice column. "I recently lost a very good friend, and the world lost a beautiful, sensitive woman of 31. After separating from her husband, she did away with herself and her two precious children. She confided her unhappiness to me a few years ago, and I let her unburden herself by the hour. It seemed to help her, but in the last few months I was out of touch with her because I was too busy to have her over. The last time we talked on the phone she said, 'Let's get together soon.' Then I put it off until it was too late.

"She needed my friendship more desperately than I knew. Many came to her funeral, but where were they when she needed them? And where was I? Wrapped up in my own little world with my own petty problems."

Most of us have this experience in one way or another: the haunting of the "might have been," the knowledge of the "too late." We have "mired" through many a sleepless hour with vain regrets. We've permitted ourselves to become ill, mentally and physically, with such grovelling.

How well our Lord is aware of this! That is evidenced

in the gospel stories when he declares to the miserable one before him, "Your sins are forgiven; go and sin no more." Our sins are buried in the deepest sea—and erased—forgotten —in his divine forgiveness! Here is the balm of Gilead for our lives.

This woman's letter points out a sin that we are most likely to commit, and least likely to be aware of or to acknowledge—the sin of omission. Think of all the things we *haven't done!*

How well Marguerite Wilkinson puts it:

> I have not cut my neighbor's throat;
> My neighbor's gold I have not stole
>   (sic):
> I have not spoiled his house or land,
> But God have mercy on my soul,
> For I am haunted night and day
> By all the things I have not done!
> O unattempted loveliness;
> O costly valor never won!

Robert Louis Stevenson echoed this: "The only sins worth thinking about are the sins of omission." And he was not too far away from echoing our Lord. The Bible teaches us that one of the very worst sins is doing nothing!

So you face this moment of truth and you wallow in vain regrets.

Is this your answer? In Psalm 51, King David pleads:

> Create a pure heart in me, O God,
>   and give me a new and steadfast
>   spirit;
> Do not drive me from thy presence
>   or take thy holy spirit from me;
> Revive in me the joy of thy deliverance
>   and grant me a willing spirit to uphold me.

What to do?

Accept God's forgiveness as you have confessed it. Ask him to guide you today to be so in his will that you can't help but be about his errands of love.

In instances where you can make amends, pray for the courage and will to do so. Do it today. And then accept the joy of deliverance and ask him to cleanse your heart of any ill-will.

Let the regrets of what you didn't do yesterday be erased by your earnest desire to be about his errands today!

Lord, if I should have to live with all the memories of things I have not done, I'd be sunk. Thank you for forgiveness. Create in me a clean heart, open to your will and directions. Help me today to be so sensitive to your will that there will not be haunting regrets. Thanks for your empowering. Amen.

The Secret of a Happy Home

If then our common life in Christ yields anything to stir the heart, any loving consolation, and sharing of the Spirit, any warmth of affection or compassion, fill my cup of happiness, by thinking and feeling alike, with the same love for one another, the same turn of mind, and a common care for unity. There must be no room for rivalry and personal vanity among you, but you must humanly reckon others better than yourselves. Look to each other's interests and not merely to your own. Let your bearing towards one another arise out of your life in Christ Jesus.

PHILIPPIANS 2:1-5

"Movie Studies Reveal U.S. Family as Joyless," reads the headline. Fifty families were filmed to study patterns of family inter-action. The survey showed that there is plenty of talk, but not much laughter. In only two families was any notable zest, any special joy in living, evident.

A sad commentary! In this affluent country, which has but 6% of the world's population, yet consumes 50 percent of the world's goods; where there are amazing educational opportunities; where toys are in such abundance as to be superfluous; where cars, boats, snowmobiles, and campers overflow garage space—in a country of such abundance most families are joyless.

Hadn't we better take inventory? What makes for joy in a home?

At the top of my list of priorities is communication, communication at the gut level of life, down where the hurts and frustrations are. In his book *Creative Brooding* Robert Raines includes a letter written by a 16-year-old juvenile delinquent boy, about to leave home. The boy writes, "Remember when I was about six years or seven and I used to want you just to listen to me? I remember all the nice things you gave me for Christmas and my birthday and I was really happy with the things about a week—at the time I got the things, but the rest of the time during the year I really didn't want presents. I just wanted all the time for you to listen to me like I was somebody who felt things too, because I remember even when I was young I felt things. But you said you were too busy."

Why don't we listen to each other? Isn't it because we are too preoccupied with ourselves?

St. Paul knows the real key: "You must humbly reckon others better than yourselves. Look to each other's interests and not merely to your own."

Think what could happen in a family if each were to live out these recommendations. Instead of wanting to pour out our tale of woes, as to how difficult the children have been and how bored we are, we homemakers would seek to be sensitive to the inner needs of both our husbands and our children. And often we would find that the surface reaction was a cover-up for a deep longing, an aching heart. What a joy, then, to be used of God as a balm in Gilead.

We need communication not only with each other in depth, but as a foundation to this relationship, we need deeper, more honest communication with God. It has become a cliche to say, "The family that prays together stays together." This is mere sounding brass if the prayers are *mere* superficial performances. But if family prayers are honest confessions of our needs and failures, and joys and accomplishments, then the clogged channels are cleared and there is a unity of spirit and togetherness that spells abundant joy.

When Christ is truly at the heart of a home, joy abounds as we become sensitive to each other's needs, and each counts the other more worthy.

Lord when our home is joyless, help us realize that it's because we haven't made room for you! Make us quick to speak our love to one another. Make us willing to confess our faults and ask forgiveness. Give us listening ears and hearts to hear you and each other. Bless our home. Amen.

On to Victory

*It is not to be thought that I have
already achieved all this. I have not
yet reached perfection, but I press on,
hoping to take hold of that for which
Christ once took hold of me. My
friends, I do not reckon myself to
have got hold of it yet. All I can say
is this: forgetting what is behind me,
and reaching out for that which lies
ahead, I press towards the goal to win
the prize which is God's call to the
life above, in Christ Jesus.*

PHILIPPIANS 3:12-14

Isn't it thrilling to see a photograph
of a mother and her child, or a father
and his growing son! This symbolizes the gift of one generation to another. How we need to keep alive this ongoing
sense of destiny in God's great plan for our lives. As the
young people sing so well today, we need to "pass it on."

It is not enough to pass on what has been given to us.
We are challenged to add our own witness, our own vision
and dreams. Can't you sense the exciting prospectus to the
Apostle Paul's words, "I press on to the goal . . . not that
I have achieved. . . ." We need to be asking ourselves the
question, "Where do we go from here?" In this generation,
with all its inventions and discoveries, how can we be a
part of God's purposes? What new dimension can we give
our lives?

I think many of the young people have set a great example. I have seen more outright dedication of lives laid on the line to serve others in Christ than I was ever aware of in my youth. I remember the selfish, sentimental songs we sang:

> With some one like you,
> a pal so good and true,
> I'd like to leave it all behind and go and find
> Some place that's known to God alone . . .
> And *let the rest of the world go by.*

For many in my youth, this was our idea of bliss. Today's word is "involvement." Put your life on the line! There is unfinished business for the King of kings. He challenges us to be about it.

But before we make a glib commitment, we should consider the cost. The Lord doesn't promise a rose garden. Thackery has said, "He who climbs a tree must grasp the branches and not the blossoms." And some of those branches can be brambled and rough. No, the Lord doesn't promise us a rose garden, but he promises the deep down joy of being in his service; the peace that comes from knowing we have obeyed him, and the fullness of his love as it flows through our heart to others.

Make no little plans. Attempt great things for God—and you will be passing on to the next generation blessings upon blessings.

I'm reminded of the District of Columbia taxi driver who was showing a tourist the sights. They passed the Archives building on which is the inscription: "The Past Is Prologue." "What does that mean?" asked the tourist. "Think nothing of it, ma'am," replied the driver. "That's government language! What it really means is, You ain't seen nuthin' yet."

Lord, my plans have been too small! Help me to think not just of my generation but of what I would pass on to the next. Give me courage and faith to dare great things for You. Thanks for the promises of your power. Amen.

The Little Things

Take us the foxes, the little foxes that spoil the vines.

SONG OF SOLOMON 2:15 (KJV)

A news item reported that many pending trials could not be held in Salonika, Greece, because mice had devoured files in the civil court archives

It called to mind a novel, *Quiet Street,* by Ossorgin. The setting was pre-revolutionary Russia. Skillfully the writer depicted generation after generation of mice in a certain home, gnawing away at the joists, until one day the floor caved in. Until then life had gone on as if nothing were happening. No one seemed aware of the rodents at work.

I am reminded of the White House incident during President Truman's time. One day the grand piano almost fell through the floor. The culprits that caused the unexpected debacle were little termites, hardly discernible to the eye.

What a telling parable this is of our lives! Unless our ears are opened to the Lord; unless our eyes see beyond the obvious; unless we seek grace to discern the things that are eternal; WHAM! Our house caves in!

What could be the "little mice" in your life? Could they be frittering away your time on non-essentials? Could they be anxieties that you haven't turned over to the Lord? Could they be "harmless" indulgences of the flesh that seem to be so inconsequential?

How about neglecting to strengthen the beams by study

26

and prayer? How about evading the gentle tapping of the Spirit to serve?

Or could it be the infection that comes from unconfessed sin or hidden resentment?

Isn't it great that the "Rock," the "Cornerstone," is untouchable, indestructible? My confirmation hymn was:

> My hope is built on nothing less
> Than Jesus' blood and righteousness.

Listen to the chorus:

> On Christ, the solid rock, I stand;
> All other ground is sinking sand.

The way to defeat the mice is to build on the Solid Rock. And in this building, little things are very important. Little deeds of kindness, a passing encouraging word, a cup of cold water in his name.

Little things can destroy but little things can also build.

Lord, the destructive things in life are so subtle. They gnaw away without our being aware. Give me discernment and courage. Help me to be aware of the little things that make life worthwhile. Be my Rock. Amen.

Afraid of Being Hurt

A man's fears will prove a snare to him, but he who trusts in the Lord has a high tower of refuge.

PROVERBS 29:25

The fear of the Lord is pure and abides for ever.   PSALM 19:9

For the spirit that God gave us is no craven spirit, but one to inspire strength, love, and self-discipline.

2 TIMOTHY 1:7

A cartoon shows two porcupines facing one another. One says, "I'd love you, but I'm so afraid of being hurt!" How true for most humans.

What a miserable prison is fear! In it, lurk horrible nightmares and wild dreams that cripple the soul and make life a hell. Jesus Christ has come to set us free from this scourge. In John 8:31-32 Jesus says, "If you dwell within the revelations I have brought you, you are indeed my disciples; you shall know the truth and the truth will set you free."

Why live life in a prison cell when there is one who wants to set you free?

Let's take a look at some of the fears that obsess us. We're afraid of the retribution for past sins. But our Lord has said, "Be of good cheer; your sins are forgiven!" We're afraid of being alone. He says, "Though your father and mother forsake you, I will never forsake you." Or we're afraid of the future! Listen to him: "Be of good cheer; I have overcome the world!" We need to take all these lurking monsters out of the dark corners of our hearts and expose them to the light of God's love!

But the fear our prickly friend in the cartoon expresses is still another fear: that of being hurt! Maybe we'd better take a long look at Jesus Christ! If he had succumbed to such a fear, where would we be?

What do we mean by "being hurt"? The analysis isn't pleasant or easy, because when we are "hurt" it simply means the "I," the ego, has been dethroned. Rest assured that hurt feelings are not experienced by those who are willing to die to self, and live for Christ. It isn't important how people react to us. Only that we become instruments of love.

But I'd better confess that it is a never-ending process. It is a constant struggle. This "I" has more lives than a cat, and even when I think it has been buried there it is again.

Dare to love, and trust God to heal any hurt.

Dare to expose yourself to other people's sorrows and problems and needs; and God will give you strength and courage and joy.

Recall those glorious lines from Philippians 2:5: "Let your bearing towards one another arise out of your life in Jesus Christ." In the same chapter, verse three has the key: "There must be no room for rivalry and personal vanity among you, but you must humanly reckon others better than yourselves."

"Nothing ventured, nothing gained," is the old saying.

In this age, God is calling us to dare to love as we have never loved before. The great anthropologist, Teilhard de Chardin has a prophetic word: "Some day, after we have mastered the winds, the waves, the tides, and gravity, we will harness for God the energies of love: then for the second time in the history of the world, man will have discovered fire."

Dare to love someone today!

Release the resistants in me, Lord, that keep me from loving as you would have me do! Clean out the pockets of fear in my life! Amen.

What Shall I Give Him?

Listen, my son, listen, and become wise; set your mind on the right course.   PROVERBS 23:19

Expecting a gift from them, the man was all attention. And Peter said, "I have no silver or gold; but what I have I give you: in the name of Jesus Christ of Nazareth, walk."

ACTS 3:5-6

A handwritten letter, folded and tucked into a blue envelope bearing the name "God" was discovered in an offering basket on the final night of an evangelism crusade. The letter read:

Dear God,

Please don't think me to be smart by putting grass in your offering plate.

It means I am giving it up for your Son, Jesus Christ. It won't be easy, but I know with help from you and a little faith, I will find peace.

Only you know how I feel. And I now realize I can't make it on my own. Please help me, God. I want to be part of your family.

I'm sorry for what I have done in the past. Give me another chance.

Thank you, God.

Your daughter, Debbie.

With the letter was a packet of marijuana wrapped in foil.

The packet of marijuana was a strange contribution to an offering plate, but what a symbol! Debbie gave up the very thing that was separating her from God. As I read about Debbie I was moved to remember her in prayer, because surely her struggle would not be easy. I prayed that God would provide Christian friends to strengthen her in her resolve, that he would open up opportunities of new friendships and service. This would give her a new "high," the kind that comes from the indwelling of the Holy Spirit.

Then I began to ask myself how willing I am to be an answer to that prayer. How willing am I to change my schedule, to give up my plans, if somebody needs me? And how cheerfully do I do it?

Another thought has haunted me since I read Debbie's letter. What do I need to put in the offering basket for the Lord? What in my life is an obstacle to the free flowing of his Spirit through my heart to the hearts of others?

Often these obstacles can be good things in themselves. They need not be dope, or alcohol, or sexual excesses. They may be pride, selfishness, self-protection, love of some person, or some thing more than we love God. Daily we need to take inventory.

I've been thinking about Peter's gift, too, as described in Acts 3. His was the gift of a helping hand. Of course there was a miracle that followed. There always is with a helping hand. It may not always show in the renewal of the body, but always it makes for a mended heart.

"But what I have, I give you."

Are you honestly willing to say that to the Lord today?

We had a Debbie experience in Switzerland when we were living there. One night we received a frantic call from a young friend attending a fashionable boarding school. She said her roommate had tried to take her life by slashing her wrists. Could they come to our house? Would we try to help?

I'll never forget those hours! Here was a brilliant young sixteen-year-old who was turned off on life. It wasn't so much to be wondered at. Her parents in Kansas were separated. Her father was a prosperous lawyer, her mother an outstanding psychiatrist. She had been sent to school in Switzerland with a car of her own, and everything money could buy. And here she was trying to take her life. Why? She felt rejected, unloved, and this made her life intolerable.

My husband spent hours of counseling as he tried to make real to her that there is a love that never would forsake her, a Heavenly Father who cares. She returned to school then, but a few weeks later the school called and asked if we would meet her at the train and put her on a plane for the United States. That short ride between conveyances was packed with prayer and loving concern.

Three months later we received as beautiful a letter from her as has ever been droped in our box. She had laid her life in God's offering basket and was finishing school, preparing for a life of service to mentally retarded children. The letter breathed gratitude and praise to God!

What will your gift to him be today?

Search me, Lord, that I may know what keeps me from being wholly yours. I want to be released from anything that binds and shackles me! Amen.

The Greatest of These . . .

I may speak in tongues of men or of angels, but if I am without love, I am a sounding gong or a clanging cymbal. I may have the gift of prophecy, and know every hidden truth; I may have faith strong enough to move mountains; but if I have no love, I am nothing. I may dole out all I possess, or even give my body to be burnt, but if I have no love, I am none the better.

1 CORINTHIANS 13:1-3

The introductory line to this sublime passage of scripture is, "And now I will show you the best way of all!"

In the paraphrase entitled, *Letters to Street Christians*, the verses following the ones we have already quoted are very plain. "If God's love is controlling you, you will be patient and kind. You won't even get jealous, won't brag about yourself, you won't be thinking about impressing people, won't have to grab at places of importance or go after things for yourself. You won't get upset by what people say and do to you or get hassled up at people who burn you. If you're being controlled by God's love, you'll be hurt to see people rip off others" (1 Corinthians 13:4-7).

Could the fruits of the Spirit who is love be spelled out more plainly?

We were entertaining some Indian friends in our home

34

in Washington, D.C. They were Hindu. I knew there were food prohibitions so I tried to be careful of what I prepared. How appreciative they were of this! As we sat about the table, our children made inquiry of their families, their homes, their native country. It was a happy time with everyone sharing. When we have an evening meal, we conclude with the breaking of spiritual bread. We don't change this pattern when guests are present. On this night, my husband chose to read 1 Corinthians 13 from the J.B. Phillips version. You should have seen the rapt expression on the faces of our guests. When he finished, they applauded. As we had our prayers, the children remembered their families back in India and asked God's blessing on them. What an experience this was! For hours afterwards we discussed the words that had been read, and shared their truths for our lives. But love had led the way for the reading.

When we think of this greatest power in all the world, as we know it incarnate in Jesus Christ, we might well ask ourselves four questions:

1. Is your home better for you? It must be either better or worse. Which is it?

2. Is your town the better for you? Are you a part of the salt that is keeping it from corruption, or are you a part of the corruption?

3. Is your land better for you? Is it the land you love? Are you then a glad Christian and a good citizen?

4. Is your world the better for you? Are you, however small, one of its lights? Would your fellows miss a big loving heart if you were called away? Will the world be poorer when you are gone?

When I read the second chapter of Philippians, I am deeply moved by what Christ did for me! The Christ, Lord of lords, King of kings—a babe in the manger, a man on the cross, for me—and all the world. And then, that he can use me to channel this love to others—that indeed is a miracle of the first magnitude.

The world needs this miracle today—in you!

The Holy Spirit, fill me with your love. Cleanse me, renew me, and send me on your errands with joy. Alleluia! Amen.

What to Remember— What to Forget

Remember, Lord, thy tender care and thy love unfailing, shown from ages past. Do you remember the sins and offenses of my youth, but remember in thy unfailing love.   PSALM 25:6-7

In the night I remember thy name, O Lord, and dwell upon thy law.

PSALM 119:55

A writer described memory quirks.

"They were playing the Della Reese record, 'Don't You Know,' on the radio and I was singing along with it and thinking that the tune of that song is an aria from 'La Boheme,' but I couldn't remember the name of the aria. And then I wasn't even sure that it was from 'La Boheme.'

"I used the last paper towel on the roll and walked across the kitchen to get a new roll and by the time I got to the cabinet I couldn't remember what I'd walked over there for."

Memory quirks are in some measure familiar to us all. Those of us upon whom the years are piling up, are acutely aware of the tricks of memory. My husband and I often have to chuckle (it's better to do this than to debate the matter!)

because we each remember the same thing with different details. And I find myself fusing one memory into another as a haziness envelopes the mind.

On the other hand, it's a remarkable thing that early memories return crystal clear through the on-going years.

The Bible has something to say about what to remember and what to forget.

Again and again we are urged to remember the mercies and loving-kindness of our God. We are also given the way that we can forget the ugly sins by coming to God to acknowledge our mistakes, to seek his forgiveness and to *accept it*. The latter is one of the hardest things for many to do. We almost take an unholy delight in wallowing in the mud of past offenses. How the devil loves to use this weapon to keep people from knowing the joy and freedom of the Lord.

I like this aptly phrased word of warning:

> Tread softly—the years roll out
> A carpet of memories for our hearts
> to walk on.

What you do today makes the memories that will bless or break you tomorrow. We must daily remind ourselves to live in the "now." And by the same token, it is a law of life that it must always move forward.

Maybe it would be good to take a look at what makes for blessed memories. Think back over your life! When you have stepped out on faith; when you have trusted God even though things looked dark; when with courage you have faced a difficult situation: aren't these times the good ones to remember?

Someone has said that one of the shortest poems in modern times is:

> Why
> Try?

Another has written:

Sitting still and wishing,
Makes no person great;
The Good Lord sends the fishing,
But you must dig the bait.

One of my favorite descriptions of faith is by Tagore, the poet from India: "Faith is the bird that feels the light and sings when the dawn is dark."

What makes for great memories? What about those times when you were motivated by God's love to be his channel to someone else? Incidentally, one of the "remembers" of scripture is to remember the poor.

And there is that remember that should tower over all else! Remember Jesus. Remember who he is, the kind of a human being he was, what he did for us! Go to the Word—and read and listen—and remember! Emulate the Mary who "hid these things in her heart" to be called to mind in a dark and cloudy day. Well did someone say, "God gave us memory so we could have roses in December."

A beloved sister-in-law, Ruth Youngdahl, has been a patient for many years in a nursing home. Two aneurysm operations in the brain crippled her memory and mental capacities. Most things she can't remember. But as we share in devotions she remembers every word of the twenty-third Psalm and of the Lord's Prayer. And as we strike up the familiar hymns, she'll join us through many verses. "Children of the Heavenly Father," "Beautiful Savior," "What a Friend We Have in Jesus," "All the Way My Savior Leads Me"—those recordings in her mind are sharp and clear. Otherwise her conversation is limited. Most amazing of all, she will say over and over again as you sit with her, "I love you. I love you." These words she remembers.

How we all need to remember Jesus Christ—and how he loves us! I like these words by Norman Habel:

I hear the tulips laugh beneath the
winter snow,

I've seen how little children make
their parents grow,
I'm sure that miracles can set the
heavens aglow,
For I believe that Christ is chang-
ing
Everything! Everything! Everything!
Everything!

The dying thief on the cross asked you to remember him, Lord. Peter remembered what you said when that cock crowed. Help me today to remember your love and mercy, and to pass them on so that they will be a beautiful memory for tomorrow. Amen

How Do
You Lie?

Put fraud and lying far from me.

PROVERBS 30:8

*Justice is rebuffed and flouted while
righteousness stands aloof; truth
stumbles in the market place and honesty is kept out of court, so truth is
lost to sight, and whoever shuns evil
is thought a madman.*

ISAIAH 59:14-15

*Out of the mouths of babes, of in-
fants at the breast, thou hast rebuked
the mighty.*   PSALM 8:2

One day the mother of ten-year-old
Lisa was called to her school princi-
pal's office. The principal explained that Lisa was responsible,
a good student, and caused no discipline problems and therefore the teachers were all the more surprised by a recent event.
Lisa claimed that she had returned a library book, but the
librarian's records showed that the book had not been returned. After a confrontation in the principal's office Lisa's
mother suspected that her daughter was lying.

She went home and searched Lisa's dresser drawers to
find it hidden in the bottom of one drawer. When Lisa returned from school her mother faced her with the truth.

"Don't you know that you must never lie, Lisa?"

41

"You and Daddy tell lies," she countered, "or just the same as lies, lots and lots of times. Why shouldn't I?

"Didn't Daddy say I was younger than I was when we took the plane to visit Grandma? And don't you sometimes say you are 31 when I know you are older? And remember the time you told Daddy your coat cost $30 less than the price on the sales tag?"

This is an example of the sickness of our age—falsifying! It is in the very fabric of our living. Some of our advertising misrepresents and misleads. Miracles are claimed for every product produced, and a gullible public spends its wherewithal on a good number of fakes. But let's not point our finger at others. Hadn't we better ask ourselves, "How truthful am I? In what insidious little ways have I prevaricated and covered over? Could it be that I have lied by some of the things I have not said, or by a look, or by innuendo?"

At another time Lisa reminded her mother of an incident in the supermarket. The checker had added wrong and charged two dollars too little. "Didn't you just laugh about that?" Lisa asked.

When her mother insisted that Lisa take the book back and confess she had lied, she admitted it would be tough. Then she added, "I'd like you to come with me to the store." So she took Lisa to the shopping center where she returned the two dollars. That was a wise and brave mother.

After some weeks of questioning I read that Watergate had cost the taxpayers $8,000,000 up to that date. What a sum to ferret out a lie that caused so many others of its own kind!

To whom do we lie, we nice people?

The Bible says we deceive *ourselves* if we say we do not sin! And we try to deceive God. In our time it is considered almost clever when you can deceive someone else.

We need to let the Lord search each of our hearts, probe into every hidden corner! He desires truth in the inward parts.

The beginnings seem so harmless: a cookie stolen from

42

the cookie jar; cheating on an examination at school; a fib to a friend—and then living a life that belies the one we claim to follow! This is the big lie against which many young people are rebelling!

How grateful I am, that the one who will be judge is the one who said, "I'm the way, the *truth*, the life!"; that with him is everlasting mercy and forgiveness to all who confess and repent. How grateful I am that he knows me as I am, and still loves me. How grateful I am that in him I am free!

Is there some half-truth you should clear up today? Is there some festering falsehood you should lance for the healing of your soul? Succinctly the Bible says, "If we confess . . . he will cleanse . . . !"

Spirit of truth, the father of lies often whispers in my ear. I know the world is full of deceit and falsehood. I may not even know it, but I am at times cast in the same role as Judas. Forgive me, Lord, and lead me to speak your truth in love. Amen.

The Healing
of the Heart

Turn to me and show me thy favor,
for I am lonely and oppressed.
Relieve the sorrows of my heart
and bring me out of my distress.

PSALM 25:16-17

My heart beats fast, my strength has
ebbed away, and the light has gone
out of my eyes.   PSALM 38:10

A beautiful devotional time could be spent in reading all the Bible has to say about an aching heart. The Scriptures have much to say about the cause of a broken heart as well as the restoration to health and stability for a wounded spirit.

One broken hearted woman shared her feelings in a letter printed in a newspaper advice column. After twenty-eight years of married life she found herself deserted by her spouse. She thought she was emotionally, physically, and financially prepared, but when the break came she went completely to pieces. "I felt I had nothing to live for. What I believed had been a disastrous marriage was heaven compared to the suffering I was now enduring. I felt there was no reason for me to clean house, shop, eat, dress up or generally take care of myself. The despair, loneliness, fright, and hurt ego took over my senses."

How many reasons for heartaches there are! What is yours? Have you been disappointed with a loved one, a friend? Are you lonely and depressed?

To all such I would plead that you call on Jesus Christ to help you. A shop in Rockford, Illinois, has this sign above the entry: "We mend everything but broken hearts!" Of the Lord it could be said, "He mends everything, *especially* broken hearts." Try him!

Then I would suggest you find a friend to whom you can unburden. God means for us to bear one another's burdens. Find someone you can trust and tell your story.

And next, find another aching heart and let God use you to be the balm of Gilead. Nothing will heal your heartache as fast as helping someone else. Try it!

If you have been spared many heartaches, pray for sensitivity to the needs of others and be the friend to whom they can come in confidence. You can be the friend whom the Lord can use as his instrument in the healing process. There is no greater joy for anyone than this! You can make the difference!

It is said of our Lord that he died of a broken heart. In Matthew 26:38 we read, "My heart is ready to break with grief. . . ." He knew what was ahead for him. Scripture records that on the way of the cross they spat on him and used the cane to beat him about the head. And of his disciples it is said, "They all deserted him." No wonder on the cross his final ignominy was in the words, "My God, my God, why hast thou forsaken me?"

He knew all this when he said to the paralyzed man let down through the roof, "Take heart, my son; your sins are forgiven." And again when the disciples were terrorized as they saw him walking on the lake and they cried out, "It is a ghost!" At once he spoke to them, "Take heart! It is I; do not be afraid!" He knew what he would be facing when he was talking to his disciples in the upper room and preparing them for what was ahead. "In the world you will have trouble. But take courage! The victory is mine; I have conquered the world!"

The message to everyone with an aching heart, "He has

healing for you!" He wants you to be his healing to all you meet. You can make the difference.

A friend related how she had come to church, burdened and heavy-hearted. Her alcoholic husband was dying in agony of soul and body. Someone that morning spoke the word of our Lord's compassion and forgiveness to this friend. The Old Testament lesson for the day was the glorious Isaiah passage, "He has sent me to bind up the brokenhearted, to proclaim liberty to captives and release to those in prison . . . to comfort all who mourn . . . a garment of splendor for the heavy heart." She told a friend as she left the service, "It's happened again—the miracle of the renewed heart!"

You've told us, Lord, to cast all our burdens on you. You've challenged us, Lord, to help others bear their burdens too. Heal us! Use us! Amen.

How Concerned Are We for the Poor?

*The spirit of the Lord God is upon
me because the Lord has anointed me;
he has sent me to bring good news
to the humble, to bind up the brokenhearted, . . . to proclaim a year of
the Lord's favor and a day of the
vengeance of our God; to comfort all
who mourn, to give them garlands
instead of ashes, oil of gladness instead of mourner's tears, a garment
of splendour for the heavy-heart.
They shall be called Tree of Righteousness, planted by the Lord for his
glory. Ancient ruins shall be rebuilt
and sites long desolate restored; they
shall repair the ruined cities and re-
store what has long lain desolate.*

ISAIAH 61:1-4

If Jesus had been running a political
campaign, this would have been his
platform. As recorded in Luke 4:18, he read these words
from the scroll in his home town synagogue in Nazareth and
declared that this scripture was fulfilled before their very
eyes.

What a platform!

It is a known fact that the Jewish people take concern for their own poor very seriously. It is a rare thing to find a Jewish person on welfare rolls. And it is amazing that the Hadassah women in Minneapolis have been contributing to Augustana congregation's emergency Relief Program as a way to express their concern for the poor.

The hikes for the hungry dramatize the need. I can only rejoice at every effort to raise funds to alleviate proverty, to provide research for diseases, to emphasize the need for compassion or concern.

But in our day we must be aware that it is not enough to offer band-aids for these wounds. If we really are to be effective we must get at the causes.

From the Christian Action Ministry in Chicago where our son and daughter invest their lives comes the story that was an early inspiration for their united efforts.

A man was fishing by the river. He was startled from his pleasing occupation by the cry of a man drowning. It seemed to come from downstream. He kicked off his shoes, stripped off his jacket, and dived in to save the man. Soon he had him up on the shore. But as he was about to put his shoes on, he heard another cry. Sure enough, another man was drowning. He repeated his rescue operation, when still a third victim was heard. It finally occurred to him that this procedure was hopeless. He'd better find out who was pushing these folks in. He needed to get at the source of the trouble.

How desperately we need to do this in today's world and in our own country. We need to get at the root causes of poverty. Then we need to join hands to eradicate them. How easy it is for those of us who have, to point out why others have not. The superpride of self-achievement fills the very air about us!

As intelligent Christians we need to be informed about real estate exploitation, scandalous rentals for rat-infested quarters, and add to this the unjust tax deductions of the rich. We need to be aware of job discrimination and the inequality of our school systems. Check on the amount spent per pupil in a poor neighborhood as compared with the average spent in an affluent area. If our democracy is really to work we must search out the causes for the disintegration of our big cities and the crime and terror that walk our streets. And we must join hands and get involved.

The name Kunstler will be like waving a red flag before some readers, but please consider a moment. You may not agree with many things, but listen to the speech he made before the Jaycees in a Minneapolis suburb. He told this group of "well-heeled" young executives that he was amazed to be invited to speak before them. It was like invading enemy territory. Then he went on to tell them that he once sat where they sat, was well up the ladder of success, had a prosperous law practice, and in his own words, "I was writing a long obituary." But he was confronted by the challenge, "What, if anything, am I doing for others? How am I contributing to justice for the oppressed?" Then came the turning point. He turned his back on material affluence and began defending the underdog. Two thirds of those present rose to their feet in applause, an unexpected demonstration.

Similar themes are developed in *The Captains and the Kings* by Taylor Caldwell, *Soul Sister* by Grace Halsell, *Whatever Became of Sin?* by Dr. Karl Menninger, and *In This Sign* by Hannah Green.

How concerned are you really about the poor? Are you willing to get involved, to inform yourself in depth, to join others in putting into practice Jesus' platform?

I've been lukewarm, Lord, to the needs of those about me, I don't want to be involved. Fire my heart with your spirit of compassion and concern for the least and the lost! Amen.

The Cancer Fear

*He went round the whole of Galilee,
teaching in the synagogues, preaching
the gospel of the kingdom, and curing
whatever illness or infirmity there
was among the people.*

*He now called the Twelve together
and gave them power and authority
to overcome all the devils and to cure
diseases, and sent them to proclaim
the kingdom of God and to heal.*

LUKE 9:1-2

Any study of scripture makes very clear that to Jesus sickness was an enemy, but an enemy that he had the power to overcome. How tremendously he has used medical science, to further this end. When I grew up tuberculosis, or consumption as it was then called, was a name to strike fear into everybody's heart. Today that disease is all but eradicated. Then there was polio with its unhappy crippling. Now the Salk vaccine has made polio cases rare indeed. So it is with measles and other infectious diseases.

Today, two of the top killers are heart disease and cancer. Great strides are being made in research but still these phantoms of fear at some time or other hover over almost every household. What difference can I make in driving away this ghost?

The first step is to take the fear out into the open and look it full in the face. Hidden anxieties can accelerate a disease.

As Christians, we wage this battle in a two-pronged offensive. First, because of Christ's resurrection and love we can say, "So what!" He has promised sufficient grace for whatever happens! And in this very release of faith, there is healing.

Second, we can cooperate in every way with the healing process offered. And as we do this, we can ask for grace to let the entire experience glorify him.

In her book, *Who's Afraid of Birthdays?* Dr. Anna Mau says, "We often hear it said, 'Where there is life there is hope!' It is even more correct to put it, 'Where there is hope there is life.' " As Christians it is our privilege to hold out this beacon of hope, no matter what may befall!

This last year has meant facing up to the implications of what I am saying in a very personal way. In the process of prostate surgery the doctors discovered that my husband had a malignancy. It came as a shock, because in his 43 years of ministry he had never missed preaching a Sunday because of illness. He had never been in a hospital except to visit others and had never really known what it was to be ill. He tells of the thoughts that went through his mind as he took the first of a long series of cobalt treatments. It was a marvel to see the skilled hands direct the huge impersonal machine which generated the powerful healing rays (misdirected, these could wreak havoc to the sound tissues). Then there was the dedicated teamwork of doctors and nurses. And enveloping all, there was the presence of the Creator of heaven and earth, and the awareness of the countless prayers being said on his behalf. In its depth, it became a hallelujah experience!

Then he related that he could identify with all the people at whose bedside he had shared the reality of faith that can transmute the rugged suffering into the gold of God's love.

Perhaps one of the most beautiful experiences of our lives was Jan Worrell Anderson's memorial service. We loved Jan, as did everyone who met and knew her. In the two and one half years we had known her she had blessed our lives beyond words! She had inspired us with the beautiful music she drew forth from the golden throat of her cello, vibrations that spoke of divine love, hope, courage, compassion! She had blessed us with her dedicated service to the unloved. She and her husband Mark were shining examples of Christ's love in action.

But ever since she was a child she had fought cancer. All of her twenty-eight years she lived with it. In the later period it took the form of mastectomy, spinal infection, lungs, and spread throughout her body. To her last breath, she glorified her Savior and put her trust in him.

I don't know why Jan wasn't miraculously healed. I only know she is now with perfect healing. She's with the Lord she loved. I also know that in her span of 28 years she witnessed more to the sustaining power of God's love than most of us do in a long lifetime of 80 or more years.

In her magnificent essay entitled, "Why There Is Evil," written just shortly before her homegoing she says, "I don't blame God for my sickness. It's the result of the infection of evil in a world that has separated itself from the Creator!" And to the question, "Well, can't God do something about all the evil in the world?" her answer is, "No, he can't, and yes, he did!" She goes on to explain how God won't force people, yet he did something in the person of his Son Jesus Christ, the fulfillment of eternal life, here, and now, and wholeness forever! The verse she herself had chosen for the theme of her memorial service was, "Whether I live or die, I am the Lord's!"

Herein is the victory!
So, who's afraid?

Remove fear, beloved Physician, and bring healing to all mankind! Amen.

What Is Your Tranquilizer?

*Be advised by me, O king: redeem
your sins by charity and your iniquities by generosity to the wretched. So
may you long enjoy peace of mind.*

DANIEL 4:27

*Be at rest once more, my heart, for
the Lord has showered gifts upon
you.*   PSALM 116:7

*Now I will lie down in peace, and
sleep; for thou alone, O Lord, makest
me to live unafraid.*   PSALM 4:8

"Best Tranquilizer Is Old Fashioned
Rocker" is the headline of an inter-
esting article. And a rocking chair *is* a great tranquilizer of
the body, depending on how you rock. In mental hospitals
I have seen patients furiously rock back and forth nonstop.
It was as if their very lives depended on the speed.

Today's world is filled with advertisements of "magic"
tranquilizers to afford an escape from the tensions and tur-
moils of our lives. There are tranquilizers for sleep and pep
pills for awakening. If you believe everything you hear and
see, you might conclude that there is a remedy for every
known and unknown ailment.

We are horrified at the tremendous rise in the use of
drugs such as marijuana and heroin, yet many of us not

only blink our eyes at it, but even support the free use of alcohol, the worst drug killer of all. An Albermarle, North Carolina, mother is a one-woman war against drunken driving. In 1968 her 11-year-old son was killed by a drunken driver who lost control of his car and swerved completely off the road to the shoulder where the boys were riding their bikes. Mark was killed. His companion Glen will walk with a limp the rest of his life. The driver was given a breathalyzer and after arrest, she was released on $2,500 bond and allowed to drive home.

Mark's mother could hardly believe her son was gone. After his death, she relates, she kept bursting into tears asking God to show her what to do! Her answer came a few days later after the funeral when the arresting officer asked her not to drop the drunken driving charge against the woman who had run down the boys. What a discouraging pursuit that was! There was one postponement after another. Meanwhile the policeman who was the witness, died. In addition, the report of the tranquilizing alcohol taken by the driver could not be entered as evidence in court because there was no way to prove conclusively how the alcohol she had taken affected her ability to drive. The final outcome was a fine of $250 and a one-year suspended sentence, plus the revoking of her license for two years.

Ever since, Mark's mother has been waging a one-woman war on drunken driving. She found that more than 50% of the deaths by traffic accidents were caused by drunken drivers. In 1973 there were 54,000 such deaths across our country, more in one year than the eleven years of bloody and horrible warfare in Vietnam.

We are a drugged society today, by pills, by alcohol, by one soporific or another. God pity us unless we find our tranquillity in him! He is the one and only answer to the problem.

What does the word "rock" suggest to you? Let the winds blow; let the waves roll; let come what may. There it is! The Lord is our rock! With him there is peace and tranquillity and rest, no matter how tumultuous the sea. Read Psalm 121 and let its deep truths anchor your soul.

There is a particular key in Daniel's words to King Nebuchadnezzer when he was called in to interpret the dream of the king. The judgment of the dream was harsh, but Daniel's final words hold hope. "Be advised by me, O King: Redeem your sins by charity and your iniquities by generosity to the wretched. So may you long enjoy peace of mind!"

Could it be that the best tranquillity of all is to be about the king's business of love? Check the state of your mind when your feet have walked in his steps, when your heart has reached out to others! Who needs any other tranquilizer than the Christ who is our peace, and joy, and love! Listen to what he says, "Peace is my parting gift to you, my own peace, such as the world cannot give. Set your troubled hearts at rest, and banish your fears. . . ." John 14:27.

I know, Lord, that you are the answer. Help me to live this knowledge every day! Amen

How Do You Search the Scriptures?

But I rely on a testimony higher than John's. There is enough to testify that the Father has sent me, in the works my Father gave me to do and to finish—the very works I have in hand. . . . But his word has found no home in you, for you do not believe the one whom he sent. You study the scriptures diligently, supposing that in having them you have eternal life; yet although their testimony points to me, you refuse to come to me for that life.

JOHN 5:36-39

The recent revival in Bible study is on the one hand thrilling, and on the other hand very frightening. I write this, knowing the danger of being misunderstood.

So I should first say that for me it is a great joy to study the scriptures. And with the Psalmist I can say in truth, "Thy word is a lamp unto my feet and a light upon my way." And, "Thy word have I hid in my heart that I might not sin against thee."

But I have been mightily disturbed by people who are well versed in scripture but who are hateful to their fellow-men. I have been amazed to discover how many there are who become "Bibleolaters," who worship the Bible more than the Christ whom it reveals. I like what Martin Luther says: "The Bible is the cradle for Jesus Christ; latent in the Old Testament and patent in the New." And the gospel of John begins with the glorious message, "When all things began, the Word already was. The Word dwelt with God, and what God was, the Word was. The Word, then, was with God at the beginning, and through him all things came to be.'

We have nitpicked over many unimportant things. Witness the split of the early church over the "yeast question" (whether or not the sacramental wafer should be leavened). We have separated and divided over non-essentials and often missed the redeeming, suffering Servant who came into the world, yearning for all to know him for now and for eternity.

What about this great upsurge of Bible study? Is it changing lives? Are we open enough to the Holy Spirit to mature and grow in our concept of God as revealed in Jesus Christ? Do we recognize him as the God of love who created all mankind and sent Jesus to redeem all?

Do our Bible studies lead us to assay our own values and priorities, our attitudes and bigotries, our selfishness and lovelessness? Or do they make us smug in our own personal salvation and judgmental of others?

The Lord has warned us about the deceptiveness of Satan. He even quotes scripture to advantage.

The Bible tells us, "By their fruits you shall know them." We should be able to expect the many who are called Christians to lead in concern for the poor, in advocacy of equal justice for all, in moral integrity and personal dedication and honesty.

There is a judgmental word in scripture that haunts me: "As it has been given to a man, the more shall be required of him." The more we study the Bible, the more God expects of us. We who know him and his word have his grace to be more loving, more compassionate, less selfish,

58

more generous, less judgmental, more forgiving; less impatient, more forebearing, less crotchety, more kind.

Do we really study the Bible so that Jesus Christ lives in us more and more?

Lord, too often I keep your words hidden in my heart, and don't let them come out and live in me. Thank you for every movement that witnesses to your power in human lives. Daily renew me in your truth! Amen.

Boredom or Abundant Living

The thief comes only to steal, to kill, to destroy; I have come that men may have life, and may have it in all its fulness. JOHN 10:10

Remember: sparse sowing, sparse reaping; sow bountifully, and you will reap bountifully. . . . And it is God's power to provide you richly with every good gift; thus you will have ample means in yourselves to meet each and every situation, with enough and to spare for every good cause." 2 CORINTHIANS 9:6, 8

Housewives bored with life are top drug users, concludes a study. They are the most frequent users of barbiturates, tranquilizers, and analgesic drugs. A significant portion are middle class housewives who are using these drugs as coping agents or as mood alteratives.

It is sad when people find life boring and take to artificial means to either stimulate or dull their God-given senses. It is particularly sad because the one who brings fulfillment and excitement and joy stands at each heart's door knocking. But the thief is also there; the thief who comes to steal and kill and destroy. Who is this thief?

As simplistic as it sounds, it is nevertheless eternally true, that thief is embodied in the one letter "I." "Navel gazing" is no new-fangled occupation. Since the beginning of time it has been man's chief foe. The "poor me" attitude, the stench of self-pity repels other people, and shuts out God.

That big "I" is the only vowel and the middle one in the word "sin." How well I remember my confirmation pastor writing those three letters on the chalkboard. Then he told us this same "I" is the blockade between us and heaven. If we permit the Holy Spirit to take hold of that "I" and bend it around until each end meets, it becomes "0"—zero, nothing. Then the transformation happens and "sin becomes son," God's Son, and as he takes over our lives, heaven enters our hearts here and now. He is also the means for the gate to be wide open to the hereafter.

What a blessing bored housewives, bored business men, bored young people could be in the lives of others! And in losing themselves in thoughtfulness to others they would be exchanging boredom for blessing. It is as simple as that.

Countless avenues of exciting opportunities for loving service are open. Churches offer them; community services are crying for help

An 81-year-old friend is finding a whole new dimension in life by enlisting himself in a remedial reading program for children. He helps an 11-year-old girl to improve her reading skills and his joy at her progress is indescribable!

Friends engaged in the "Meals on Wheels" program tell of their joy as they not only fill a physical need but in so doing, say to housebound people, "Someone cares; someone cares and loves you!"

Today, ask the Lord to guide you to someone who needs you and you will know abundant living.

My miserable times, Lord, have been the "poor me" times. Forgive me! Make me sensitive to the needs of others: to the needs of my own family, my neighbors, my communi-

ty, and to all the world. Move me away from self-preoccupa-
tion to become the channel for your healing, restoring pres-
ence to others. Do it today! Amen.

What Is Beauty?

Your beauty should reside, not in outward adornment—the braiding of the hair, or jewelry, or dress—but in the inmost center of your being, with its imperishable ornament, a gentle, quiet spirit, which is of high value in the sight of God. 1 PETER 3:3-4

Charm is a delusion and beauty fleeting; it is the God-fearing woman who is honored. PROVERBS 31:30

Miss Black America of 1973 has a message for the women and men of the world! "Beauty that lasts is from within; it is spiritual!" How refreshing a pronouncement from a beauty queen. Women are wearing themselves out fighting the battle of birthdays! Cosmetic firms cater to women's worry about aging in ads like this: "Do you realize there is a potion that may well begin the age of agelessness for women? This cream is dedicated to the exciting woman who spends her lifetime living up to her potential!"

And lest the men think they are excluded, one firm advertises false hair that can be glued to the chest of a man who wants to look virile in bathing trunks. It is guaranteed not to come off in the water.

Who are the beautiful people?

I think of Esther. After her regular working hours she brings joy and love into the children's ward of General Hospital. I think of Ethel who with her autoharp and God-given voice changes the climate of many a convalescent home. I think of Theander who uses his car as God's taxi, transporting people who otherwise would find it difficult to get out and I think of another Esther, up in years, who pours her love into the lives of little inner city children, and who with her husband tramps through rain or snow to visit the needy and housebound.

What qualities make a person beautiful? Are you more concerned about what your body is going to wear than how your soul is clothed? Do you hang the giant share of your salary on your back?

The Lord made his standard of judgment very clear when he said to Samuel, "The Lord does not see as man sees; men judge by appearances but the Lord judges by the heart."

When I was leading Bible studies at the women's reformatory of Washington, D.C., I was startled the first time I heard the women sing this song as they returned to their cells:

> Let the beauty of Jesus be seen in
> me;
> All His wondrous compassion and
> purity
> O Thou Savior divine; all my nature
> refine.
> Let the beauty of Jesus be seen in
> me.

Scripture puts it this way: "The King's daughter is all glorious within!"

Forgive, Lord, our distorted values that put costly price-tags on the cheap and cheap on the costly; get us off this kick about outward appearance, and by your Spirit cultivate within us the beauty that comes from your indwelling. Amen.

The Need
for Quiet

Be still and know that I am God.

PSALM 46:10 (KJV)

He leadeth me beside the still waters.
He restoreth my soul.

PSALM 23:2-3 (KJV)

We live in a noisy world. All the mechanical equipment and devices we use pollute the air with their noisy, whirring machinery. Doctors tell us there is a real danger to our hearing because of all the noises to which we are subjected.

It is interesting that the dictionary associates noise with nausea. Among its definitions: "Any loud, discordant, or disagreeable sound." Nausea is described as "a feeling of sickness at the stomach with an impulse to vomit!" Today's world is filled with noise to the point of our being sick and we need to recapture the joy of quietness.

I remember with shame how as a little girl when I didn't want to hear my mother's voice. I'd sing loudly or pretend I was practicing on the piano! Isn't this what many of us do with God? We invite the noises of the world to drown him out.

Our Creator knew this would be our temptation so in his Word he advises us as to our need of quiet times. The Jerusalem Bible translates Psalm 46:10, "Pause a while and know that I am God." And the New English Bible translates verses 2 and 3 of Psalm 23, "And leads me beside the waters of peace; he renews life within me."

How desperately we need these places and times of quiet! Frayed nerves and anxiety sickness are characteristic of our times! God is calling us to be still—and know him: know that he loves us, know that he is aware of our burden; know that he will bear it; know that he will never leave us or forsake us.

Do you have a quiet place and time when you listen to him? One day a stranger came to the house and rang the doorbell. A little boy answered, "May I see your mother?" the stranger asked. "Well," was the reply, "You may if you'll wait a while. She is in there praying, and I won't disturb her, because she's different when she comes out."

Lord, give me the grace and judgment each day, so to withdraw from the noise of the world as to be able to hear your voice! Silence me within, Lord, because sometimes my heart can be so noisy. Make me aware again, that you will keep me in quiet peace if my mind is stayed on you! Make this such a time, Lord. Amen.

Are You Pessimistic or Hopeful?

*So I came to hate life, since every-
thing that was done here under the
sun was a trouble to me; for all is
emptiness and chasing the wind.*

ECCLESIASTES 2:17

*Why stand so far off, Lord, hiding
thyself in time of need? The wicked
man in his pride hunts down the
poor; may his crafty schemes be his
own undoing!*
*He says to himself, 'God has forgot-
ten; he has hidden his face and seen
nothing.'*   PSALM 10:1-2, 11

*In the world you will have trouble.
But courage! The victory is mine; I
have conquered the world.*

JOHN 16:33

A poll of Minnesota residents in
1974 reported that 56 percent were
pessimistic about the world's future. The newspaper article
reported that some who were hopeful based their optimism
on their faith in God and in their fellow men. Today, and
in Bible times, people have responded to events either in despair or hope.

In our scripture readings above we find these two perspectives. The prophet Jeremiah is a shining example of despair and hope. He could never believe that national ruin was the end. True, he could see no human cause to hope, but he never lost hope because he never lost God.

The apostle Paul shows us the steps: tribulation works patience, and patience, experience, and experience, hope. In the New English translation, the meaning becomes even more clear. "More than this: let us even exult in our present sufferings, because we know that suffering trains to endure, and endurance brings proof that we have stood the test, and this proof is the ground of hope. Such a hope is no mockery, because God's love has flooded our inmost heart through the Holy Spirit he has given us" (Romans 5:3-5).

Do you witness to the world that your hope is in God? How real is your faith? How quickly does it get washed out by defeat and despair?

One instance in Thomas Edison's life tells of an assistant marveling at the bewildering total of experiments that failed. For instance, fifty thousand experiments were performed before he could develop a new storage battery. "Results," exclaimed Edison. "Why man, I have gotten a lot of results. I know several thousand things that won't work."

Listen to the words of some of the great Christians of the age in which I have lived. "The kingdom of God will not come in a day; it will not be left with the morning milk" (S. Parks Cadman). "We cannot live the way we have been living without having the kind of world we now have" (E. Stanley Jones). "The kingdom of God waits upon the radical reconstruction of human hearts known as repentance" (Ilion T. Jones). "We can have a world of peace, justice, happiness, the kingdom of God as soon as we want it. Every new scientific discovery can bend to aid humanity if people will love Christ and one another. But we must pay a price" (Frank C. Laubach)

The renowned scientist, Albert Einstein, backs up this statement of Dr. Laubach: "Our real problem is in the hearts and minds of men. It is not a problem of physics but of ethics. It is easier to denature plutonium (another fission agent discovered since uranium) than to denature the evil spirit of man. Man's skills have outstripped his morals. His engineering has leaped ahead of his wisdom. We cannot cancel or call back his scientific advance, but we can, and must, if the world is to survive, help man to catch up. In God's name, if you still believe in God, take him seriously, and somehow get control of what science has given to the world, or else—or else we shall all likewise perish."

Hope begins with you, as you take inventory of your values, of your purpose in life, of what you bring to your community and your world.

What a challenge there is in the story of a Russian youth who had become a conscientious objector to war through the reading of Tolstoy and the New Testament. He was brought before a magistrate. With strength of conviction he told the judge about the life which loves its enemies, which does good to those who despitefully use it, which overcomes evil with good and which refuses and rejects war.

"Yes," said the judge, "but you must be realistic. It's the kingdom of God you are talking about and that hasn't come yet." The young man looking the judge in the eye said, "Sir, I recognize that it has not come for you, nor yet Russia or the world. But the kingdom of God has come for me! I cannot go on hating and killing as though it had not come."

Are you willing to be a part of the answer of the hope we have in Jesus Christ? Do you meet each discouraging situation with the glimmer, "But God . . . ?" I am reminded of that worker in the ghetto with all its wretchedness who went about giving hopeful solutions to each situation always with a toss of his head to objectors and then this word, "But God is about!" Why not quietly, deep within your soul as you read this, offer yourself to him that his light of hope for this life and eternity may shine clearly in your life and words!

How about taking a poll of your own reactions?

No matter what, Lord, I believe that yours is the final victory! Use me to bring this message of hope to everyone I meet. Remind me daily, that of your kingdom there shall be no end. Let me say the words of the young Russian and say them with conviction, "But the kingdom of God has come for me!" Amen.

Show Me
Your Tongue

*I said: I will keep close watch over
myself that all I say may be free from
sin.*   PSALM 39:1

*Whoever loves life and would see
good days must restrain his tongue
from evil and his lips from deceit.*

1 PETER 3:10

*A man may think he is religious, but
if he has no control over his tongue,
he is deceiving himself.*   JAMES 1:26

Scripture uses strong words when it
speaks of the tongue. In James 3:5-6
the tongue is called a small member, but one that can make
huge claims. The contrasting uses of the tongue are pictured
in Proverbs 12:18: "Gossip can be as sharp as a sword, but
the tongue of the wise heals." Again in Proverbs 15:4 we
read, "A soothing word is a staff of life, but a mischievous
tongue breaks the spirit!" And we are warned in Proverbs
21:23 to keep a guard over our lips and tongue and keep
ourselves out of trouble.

A team of biologists at the University of Pennsylvania
has completed a five-year study of how people use their
tongues at the unconscious level. Their major finding is that
the unconscious display of the tongue is a universal sign
of aversion to social encounter, a sign that is used by all

races and nations of people. The tongue says things even when it doesn't use words!

Remember when you were ill as a child and the doctor was called? It seems to me the first thing he said was, "Show me your tongue!" Apparently the tongue is a telltale weather-vane for the climate of our body.

Scripture would have us know that it also reflects the health of mind and heart. The Lord spoke some strong words when he said, "A man is not defiled by what goes into his mouth, but by what comes out of it." What does your tongue say about you when it is talking about other people? Are you as quick to speak words of praise as you are to criticize? Do you as readily encourage as you condemn? Is your tongue like a chameleon, changing color to match its environment and reflecting what's acceptable to those around you? Is it like the tongue of an old, worn shoe, loose and quick to wag? Are you silent at the right times?

How much real silence do we experience today? Even in church when time is set aside for silent prayer, it is often made ineffective by organ music in the background.

James Porter of Ripley, Tennessee, thought he would try to save his townspeople from at least 15 minutes of radio chatter and noise so he bought up that much time on the local radio. The station was inundated with calls from listeners who didn't hear the opening remarks: "Friends, are you tense, nervous, jittery? You have tried other stations without success. Now we offer you an amazing new discovery: instant silence!" Then followed thirteen minutes of silence broken only by the announcements, to assure listeners that their sets were in order. Do you know how to find silence and use it?

Then there is the misunderstanding because words can have different meanings. A mother eagerly awaited the return of her son from his first day at school. When he came home he looked rather glum. She asked, "What's the matter? Didn't you like it?"

"Naw," he replied, "I didn't like it at all. The teacher told a lie!"

"Now, Tommy," said the mother, "I'm sure that isn't true. How can you say that she told a lie?"

"Well," was his response, "When I came in I asked her where I should sit, and she said, 'sit over there for the present.' I sat there all morning and she never gave me a present!"

What a descriptive turn of phrase we find in Psalm 126: "When the Lord turned the tide of Zion's fortune, we were like men who had found new health. Our mouths were full of laughter and our tongues sang aloud for joy." And St. Paul in his letter to the Philippians speaks of every tongue confessing the Lord.

Are the seeds of kindness, of compassion, of understanding, of hope sown by your tongue? Do your words bless or burn?

If you have a sick tongue, you'll need to call the great Physician. He is the only one who has the power to cure it.

How careless I am, Lord, with my words. I bandy them about so glibly. And sometimes they are barbed and tipped with cyanide to hurt and kill! Help me, Loving Father, to use my tongue to glorify you! Amen.

Does Your Love Show?

My children, love must not be a matter of words or talk; it must be genuine, and show itself in action.

1 JOHN 3:18

If God thus loved us, dear friends, we in turn are bound to love one another. . . . God himself dwells in us if we love one another; his love is brought to perfection within us.

1 JOHN 4:11-12

Have no fear, little flock; for your Father has chosen you to give you the Kingdom. Sell your possessions and give in charity. Provide for yourselves purses that do not wear out, and never failing treasures in heaven, where no thief can get near it, no moth destroy it. For where your treasure is, there will your heart be also (Luke 12:21-34).

Love and giving are twins. Yet there is this strange paradox: if you love, you must give; but you can give without love.

"Show your love with a heart that's real." reads an ad for gold heart-shaped pendants. Do those who give these extravagant baubles really give prompted by love?

What motives, other than love, are there for giving?

I have found myself giving because I wanted someone to think well of me. I always have to ask myself if this is what motivates my giving!

There are those who give in order to receive reciprocal favors. I remember how careful my brother was, both as governor of Minnesota and as Federal District judge, about accepting gifts. He didn't want to be obligated politically to anybody. He wanted to be free in the performance of his duties. Once two beautiful Chinese vases were delivered to his home from someone whose name he didn't recognize. He wouldn't rest until they were returned.

Some give to win God's favor. "Look, Lord, what I've given to charity," we may say, even if it's only a tip.

Some give to ease their conscience. Giving can be a covering for extravagances.

There are those who give grudgingly out of duty. They are the ones who often say, "The church is always asking for money!"

O for the joy of those who give because they love! They don't ask, "How much do I have to give?" They ask, "How little do I need for myself?"

A member of Bethel Church on the west side of Chicago, where our son David serves, is a beautiful example of giving. She has 13 children to support and earns $100 a week. Yet every Sunday she offers ten dollars in her envelope. One Sunday when we were visiting there, she had left her purse in the choir room. She had just cashed her weekly check. Her purse was stolen! Yet she remained for the Bible study after the service. This woman of faith and love kept her cool in spite of the fact that at this point she was penniless. Another beautiful part of this story is that as friends heard about her loss, they contributed out of their small salaries until the entire sum was made up. Christian love in action!

How quickly the first glow of love can wear off in marital relations! Someone has facetiously penned a before and after:

> Two lovers walking down the street!
> She trips; he murmurs, "Careful,
> Sweet!"

Now wed they tread the self-same
street;
She trips; he growls, "Pick up your
feet!"

Real love from the heart grows rather than diminishes.
How do we show it in our home? In our community?

We were overwhelmingly thrilled one Christmas by a
long distance telephone call from Indonesia, 22,000 miles
away. Our daughter and family in Djakarta had called to
ask how Grandpa was! We were practically speechless at
the joy of it. Each talked to us—except ten-year-old Karl.
We missed his boyish voice on the telephone.

A week later Biz explained in her letter. He was overcome with tears. When his sobs quieted finally, Biz asked
him to try and explain why he wept so. He slipped into his
room, and finally came out and then said to his mother,
"There were three reasons. First, Grandpa and Grandma
and all my uncles and aunts gave me so much and I have
nothing to give back. Second, I cried because my grandpar-
ents in Germany are dead. And I cried when I thought of
the summer spent at Sand Lake Cabin with Grandpa and
Grandma and all my cousins."

His mother talked with him and proposed that he make
something to send us. He and his sister Inga made an amazing calendar for us. Then she asked him what he thought
would make Grandpa and Grandma the happiest of all!
Together they decided it would be if he would give his heart
to Jesus. That, he said, he wanted to do!

Gold, diamonds, sapphires? The Lord says, "Give me
your heart!"

*What are my motives for giving, Lord? Search out my
heart! I would put my life on your altar! I love you! Amen.*

Children
and God

*Hear, O Israel, the Lord is our God,
one Lord, and you must love the
Lord your God with all your heart
and soul and strength. These commandments which I give you this day
are to be kept in your heart; you
shall repeat them to your sons, and
speak of them indoors and out of
doors, when you lie down and when
you rise.* DEUTERONOMY 6:4-7

When parents say they do not want
to impose any religious influence on
their children, but will let them choose for themselves when
they are grownups, I *shudder*. What an inconsistency! The
omission of any positive faith is as strong an influence as
any could be.

In the same breath we would say that a child cannot
inherit faith. There are no grandchildren of God, only sons
and daughters. And at a point in our lives, or all along the
way, as mature individuals we choose to accept Christ, to
reject him, or to be indifferent to him. But what a difference
parental influence makes, or the living witness of any Christian!

In a delightful book entitled *Religion for Little Children*, Dr. Brusselmans suggests specific answers to religious
questions most often asked by pre-school children. To the
question, "Who is God?" she answers, "God is someone who
knows you by your name because he loves you. You are

78

very special to him. He knows each of us by name and he loves us all. . . . He is pleased when we call him by name. He has many names . . . a beautiful one is God our Father."

Another question children ask: "Where is God?" she answers: "God is everywhere. . . . God is in every place where there is life. . . ."

In another little book, *Children's Letters to God,* the compilers share the thinking of some children. The opening commitment is terse and to the point. Herbie writes, "Dear God, count me in!" Little Sylvia poses the question related to women's lib. She writes, "Dear God, are boys better than girls? I know you are one but try to be fair."

Something of a child's faith is demonstrated in this letter from Morton: "To God. Dear sir, the reason I am writing this. My mommy and I are going to spend Easter with Aunt Bea. My daddy can't come. We are supposed to fly but my mommy is scared to go. Maybe you better come with us!"

And Mike poses a question, "Dear God, what is it like when you die? Nobody will tell me. I just want to know, I don't want to do it." He signs himself, "Your friend!"

How do you teach children about death? In the honest faith by which you live; in the resurrection promise and hope in Christ; in the words of scripture: "I go to prepare a place for you." Jesus says, "I am the resurrection and the life. He who believes in me, though he die, yet will he live."

When my brother Reuben died, I received an illustrated letter from our 7-year-old granddaughter Kris. She wrote, "I wish he did not die. But he went to be with Jesus and that is good. I loved uncle Reuben but I am happy that he went up with God."

And the ease with which children accept the things of faith is illustrated in the prayer of our daughter Mary, when she was four years old. We had been praying for a woman in our congregation who had cancer. Mary's prayer was: "Dear God, bless Grandma Anderson. And I kind of think you ought to take her home to be with You, Lord, she's suffered so long, but anyhow she's with you now, and she'll be with you then, so it really doesn't make any difference."

Help us, Lord, to be honest with children about the things of faith. Help us not to evade the questions they ask. Help us to test our own faith as we answer. Teach us to learn from them. Thank you for the example of taking them in your arms and blessing them. Amen.

Have You Ever Murdered Anyone?

You have learned that our forefathers were told, "Do not commit murder; anyone who conmmits murder must be brought to judgment." But what I tell you is this: Anyone who nurses anger against his brother must be brought to judgment. If he abuses his brother, he must answer for it to the court; if he sneers at him he will have to answer for it in the fires of hell."

MATTHEW 5:21-22

Is this a wild question, "Have you murdered anyone?" Not if we study Jesus' interpretation of the commandment, "Thou shalt not kill." Who can escape the insight of his judgment?

A 54-year-old woman was arrested after a detective posing as a hired killer said she had offered him $5,000 to murder her ex-husband. We are horrified by such a story. What human being could possibly hire someone to kill?

Let's not be so smug! Jesus says anyone who nurses anger against his brother shall be in danger of judgment. I'm sure our Lord understands our humanity, how easily anger can flare up. But here he speaks of *nursing* anger. There's a difference. In the one instance there is the flareup and then the ashes. But in the nursing process you feed the flame until it becomes quite all-consuming. Isn't our Lord talking about that human weakness of carrying a grudge? Our Lord tells us that our gifts to him are unacceptable if we know our brother has something against us. In other words, whatever might be clogging the channel between anyone and us we ought to clear. And he says plainly that hating anyone is the seed of murder. So before his throne we stand guilty if we have allowed ourselves this luxury of the devil.

In what guise are we murderers? Have we heard about looks that kill? Have we been disdainfully looking on someone whose outward appearance repels you, or whose lack of intellect disgusts us?

What is our attitude to the beleaguered minorities? How do we look at people of another color or culture?

And what a killer the tongue is, murdering reputations with the whispered, "Have you heard . . . ?" Or laying low someone's spirit with scathing words.

Do we have any sense of our own guilt in this matter? God is asking us to take a look at ourselves and let the searing white light of his judgment pierce itself into every crevice of our heart! Is there someone against whom you hold a grudge? Is there someone of whom you think ill, or who thinks ill of you? Quit nursing the infection. Pray about it and God will lead you to go to the person and clean out the festering. What we really need is a good look at ourselves as God sees us.

A woman complained to a friend who was visiting her about what a poor housekeeper her neighbor was. "Why, just look," she said, "at those clothes on her line. There are black streaks running up and down her pillow cases and sheets!" The friend stepped to the window and raised it. "It appears, my dear," she said, "that the streaks are on your window. The sheets are perfectly clean."

Holy Spirit, search out the innermost recesses of my heart for the seeds of murder. Give me the courage today to make right my relationship with . . . . Help me to see how I am at fault, and then assure me of forgiveness. Thank you that you never give me up! Amen.

Longing for the Holy Spirit

*As the hind longs for the running
streams so do I long for thee, O God.
With my whole being I thirst for
God, the living God.*   PSALM 42:1-2

In every heart, I believe there is a
yearning for God. In the time of the
psalmist's writing, there were underground watercourses
which the deer could hear and smell but not see or reach.
Often he would frantically follow this sound, hoping to find
its source. The King James version reads, "As the hart panteth after the water brooks, so panteth my soul after thee, O
God." Often people do weird things and follow strange paths
in their effort to assuage this thirst. Francis Thompson in his
poem, "The Hound of Heaven" describes mankind's search:

> I fled him down the nights and down
> > the days;
> > I fled him down the arches of the
> > years:
> I fled him down the labyrinthine
> > ways
> > Of my own mind, and in the mist
> > of tears
> I hid from him, and under running
> > laughter . . .
> > From those Strong Feet that fol-
> > lowed, followed after.

These are the nudgings of the Spirit. God in his infinite love has taken the first step to us, long before we inch our way to him. Somewhere in the depth of every living soul there is this longing.

After Miss Sullivan had established a means of communication with Helen Keller, she felt she wanted to tell her about God. The young girl's spirit rose as she said, "I know him! I know him! I didn't know his name." In our search for more knowledge and wisdom about the Holy Spirit we need to recognize that our fellow men are objects of his love and longing even as we are. If we were more sensitive to this fact, we would help make a bond to unite mankind.

In everyone you see or meet today, you look beyond the exteriors of appearance, of status, of intellect, of age, of race, or nationality, and see a soul longing for God. The Holy Spirit will help you.

Open my heart to your Spirit, O Lord, that I may accept all others as people whom you created and redeemed. Amen.

What Is Gold?

The fear of the Lord is pure and abides forever. The Lord's decrees are true and righteous every one, more to be desired than gold, pure gold in plenty. PSALM 19:9-10

And Peter said: "I have no silver or gold; but what I have I give you: in the name of Jesus Christ of Nazareth, walk!" ACTS 3:6-7

The old story of King Midas still makes a point in our times. Midas was given a wish and he wished everything he touched would turn into gold.

It was fun when he touched his chair and it became gold. Was it as much fun when he touched the roses on the bush? And it was disconcerting, to say the least, when he tried to eat, and his touch on the food turned it to gold. Of course the climax came when his little daughter came running to him, and at his touch, she became hard, cold gold.

In his Word, the Lord sets up a norm of values. The psalmist speaks to it: "The fear of the Lord and the Lord's decrees . . . are more to be desired than gold." The 28th chapter of Job contains a discourse on values: "But where shall wisdom be found . . . , the gold and the crystal cannot equal it; and the exchange of it shall not be for fine jewels of gold." Psalm 111 tells us that the fear of the Lord is the beginning of wisdom.

So often those of us who don't have much of the world's gold, look with longing eyes on those who do. Smugly we say, "Well, if I had his wealth." What a stench in the nostrils of God!

Are we able to say to the needy about us what Peter said to the lame man: "What I have I give you!"? Do you give what you have of yourself, your love, your understanding, your compassion to others?

There is a false philosophy today that says, "If you follow the Lord, you'll prosper." O yes, you'll prosper all right—in the things of the Spirit. But following the Lord may also mean losing your job, rather than compromising. It might mean trusting him even when the bottom seems to have fallen out of everything. Yet the Lord never forsakes us!

A friend of ours had to make a choice that cost him his job. His boss asked him to fill out tax forms for the company. Ernie noticed that he was expected to include an item of $75,000 for repairs. He said to his superior, "This is a mistake. We've made no such repairs." The boss replied, "You do it or it's your job." Ernie replied, "It's my job or my conscience. I live with the latter. I'll give up my job."

For months his wife and he literally lived on faith, with just enough to keep them going. Then in another town a job opportunity opened. Today, in his reflective years, he thanks God he didn't weaken. He says those lean months witnessed to God's sustaining power.

Esau sold his birthright for a mess of pottage. The temptation comes to every life in one form or another.

Faith, hope, love: these are the gold of the Spirit not to be bought or sold, but to be received as a gift from a loving Father and Redeemer.

"Seek first the kingdom. . . ." Do you?

This matter of values, Lord, comes up in everything. You know my thoughts, how I'd like a lot of gold to slosh around. You know, too, that I'd be more of a heel than I am now. Help me to recognize real gold in others and let the shimmering gold of your presence dominate my life. Amen.

Spiritual Pruning

I am the real vine, and my Father is the gardener. Every barren branch of mine he cuts away; and every fruiting branch he cleans, to make it more fruitful still.   JOHN 15:1-2

In all this, remember how critical the moment is. It is time for you to wake out of sleep. . . . It is far on in the night; the day is near. Let us therefore throw off the deeds of darkness.

ROMANS 13:11-12

The third chapter of Ecclesiastes says, "For everything its season, and for every activity under heaven its time."

Our headlines have to do with the world of nature. But God's perfect inexorable laws apply as well in the spiritual world. From his word I hear him clearly say to me, "Now is the time."

My greatest regrets in life are because I have postponed doing things for others until it was too late. Some of life's saddest words are "might have been!" But we are challenged by events in our lives to do something that is timely every day: the pruning away of those things that keep us from bearing the fruit we should.

Pause a moment, and ask the Lord to show you what to cut. He tells me I'd better get rid of the branch of irritation about the little things. How quickly I can become impatient with others! How readily I make excuses for myself!

Again and again he has shown me that the branch of anxiety is a hindrance to my fruit-bearing: anxiety about my husband's cobalt treatments (what would happen to me if something should happen to him?), anxiety about our children, each in their particular point of need; anxiety about our church, our country, the world. I'm encumbered with many of these dead branches.

There has been wormy fruit because of the branch of ill will and resentment. Carrying a grudge is a devastating branch. It can infect every other branch on the tree unless it is cut off. Then there is the branch of spiritual pride and judgmentalism. That branch is a cancer.

These are some of the things the Vine has been saying to me. And daily he says, "Now is the time to prune!"

The pruning process in my life is everlasting, Lord. The dead branches keep coming back again and again. Give me grace to cut out those things that keep me from bearing the fruits of love! Amen.

Can Others Tell You Are a Christian?

Why do you call me, "Lord, Lord"
—and never do what I tell you?

LUKE 6:46

In Urbana, Illinois, 11,000 Christian young people gathered to consider what it means to be a Christian. Certainly, no one denies that the basis is to acknowledge and accept Jesus Christ as Lord and Savior. But the young people were concerned that many of us who claim to accept Christ don't show it in our lives. Their graffiti board was telltale. One question was, "If God seems far away, guess who moved?"

But this was the most telling interrogation: "If you were arrested for being a Christian, would there be enough evidence to convict you?"

What would such evidence be?

Of our Lord, it was said, "He eats with publicans and sinners!" Can that be said of you? Or do you live securely in the comfort of "your kind" of people? When have you opened your heart and your home to the stranger in your midst, to the alcoholic, to the person out of prison, to your enemy? We all need to hear Jesus say, "Why call me Lord, Lord—and never do what I tell you?"

Do you put the most charitable construction other people's actions, and withhold judgment? Are you filled with compassion that leads to action for the underprivileged, the minorities, the poor?

Or how about your giving? In court would it be said: "Why this one gives away all that he has?"

or

"This one is no respecter of persons"

or

"This one chooses to obey God rather than the expediency of pleasing man."

or

"This one believes in the foolishness that love can redeem people. He preaches justice and mercy, when all we need is law and order."

What would you look like in court facing the accusation of being a Christian?

Jesus has some hard words for pretenders. There is nothing against which he spoke so harshly as hypocrisy. "You are like tombs covered with whitewash; they look well from outside, but inside they are full of dead men's bones and all kinds of filth" (Matthew 23:27).

We were privileged to share with some university students on the campus where our son was a chaplain. I'll never forget the young man who turned his earnest eyes on me (he was a Zen-Buddhist student) and said, "All we ask is that you put your 'bod' where your mouth is." We heard another voice, "Why call me Lord, Lord—and never do what I tell you?"

Forgive, Lord, please forgive the lack of real commitment in my life. I am so ready to receive your "comforts" and so slow to hear your "go." Help me to see my life from the eyes of the casual observer. Is there enough evidence to convict me of being a Christian? Help me, Lord! Amen.

War or Peace

*The people who walked in darkness
have seen a great light; light has
dawned upon them, dwellers in a
land as dark as death. . . . For thou
hast shattered the yoke that burdened
them, the collar that lay heavy on
their shoulders, . . . All the boots of
trampling soldiers and the garments
fouled with blood shall become a
burning mass, fuel for fire. . . .*

ISAIAH 9:2-5

The pursuit of the Cold War from 1947 to 1971 cost United States citizens the staggering sum of one trillion dollars. But the magnitude of hidden costs staggers the most vivid imagination: the countless devastated homes, burned-out villages, numberless maimed bodies, to say nothing of the souls and minds that have been warped! What is the answer? What can Christian people in a democracy do?

God is calling us to be concerned citizens, to search out facts, to become involved. How can we justify the disproportionate amount spent on weapons to kill, with the tiny amount spent on efforts to build and help?

Because I love my country and want it to be an example to the world that faith in a living God and love for everyone can make the difference between night and day, because I have this dream as enunciated in the Book of Isaiah, I dare to speak out. If enough of us would, the budget expenditures would indeed change.

In Isaiah 2 we read that the Lord will be judge among the nations. "They shall beat their swords into mattocks and their spears into pruning knives; nation shall not lift sword against nation nor ever again be trained in war!" In this same chapter we read that all men's proud achievements shall be brought low, "And the loftiness of man shall be humbled and the Lord alone shall be exalted on that day."

What do you know about your government? Do you exercise your right as a citizen to have your voice heard? How concerned are you about basic honesty in high places and low? For what would you want your country to be best known?

Read carefully the following quotation: "Every gun that is made, every warship launched, every rocket fired signifies, in the final sense, a theft from those who hunger and are not fed, those who are cold and are not clothed. This world in arms is not spending money alone. It is spending the sweat of its laborers, the genius of its scientists, the hopes of its children. This is not a way of life at all in any true sense. Under that cloud of war, is a humanity hanging on a cross of iron."

Who said it? You may be surprised to know it was Dwight D. Eisenhower, on April 16, 1953, in an address to the American Society of Newspaper Editors.

"For a boy has been born to us . . . and he shall be called . . . Prince of Peace," says Isaiah in chapter 9.

He it is, who said to his disciples, "Put up your sword. All who take the sword die by the sword."

Will you follow him?

Give us courage as citizens, Lord, to put our trust in you! Amen.

Is Resignation the Answer?

So I came to hate life, since every-
thing that was done here under the
sun was a trouble to me; for all is
emptiness and chasing the wind.

ECCLESIASTES 2:17

I know there is nothing good for man
except to be happy and live the best
life he can while he is alive. I know
that whatever God does lasts forever;
to add to it or subtract from it is
impossible.

ECCLESIASTES 3:12, 14

Everyone sensitive to the public pulse is aware of the spirit of resignation, the greyness of the pervading mental attitude. It is symbolized by the shrug of the shoulder and the colorless retort, "So what!" Bomb-shattered Europe was gripped by it in the post-war years of the late forties. Each of us in our own lives must have faced times like this when our basic response was, "What's the use?"

"We're looking to ourselves," announces a headline. No wonder things seem hopeless! But do not misunderstand! The Greeks had a significant saying, "The unexamined life is not worth living." An honest look at ourselves can be a very healthy thing, but if we focus on our own inadequacies the bugles will all be silenced.

But there is God, God revealed in Christ, who towers over the saber-rattlers of history and the kingdoms which wax and wane. There is the Christ who shines in the darkness of the world's night and through the grayness of its dawn and who is saying to each one, "Be of good cheer; I have overcome the world."

We were in Cologne, Germany shortly after the devastating war of the forties. Our Christian host related to us the despair and hopelessness that had shrouded that city. There were mountains of rubble everywhere. Then someone began to dream of rebuilding and restoring, beginning with the cathedral. They brought up the priceless stained glass windows from the deep cellars where they had been hidden. Citizens carried these and the adornments of altarware in a procession with a crucifier leading the march as they returned them to the great edifice. They sang the great hymns of faith as they marched. And then the miracle happened! Hope was born out of the ashes and rebuilding began in earnest. Only hope in a conquering Christ could produce such a result.

Our daughter and one of our sons work in the riot-torn sector of Chicago where everything seems utterly hopeless. But the churches banded together believing that in Christ, nothing is ever too hard. They call their operation the Ash Flower, for out of the ashes, Christian love has nourished up the flower of hope.

A second chance academy for high school dropouts has brought hope to hundreds of youth. Sixty-five percent of their graduates go to college.

A public health program is bringing healing and preventive measures to a community that was left without medical care. Child development centers are giving opportunities to little children who otherwise would be on the streets.

This is just a glimpse into the many-faceted program sponsored by churches banded together under CAM (Christian Action Ministry).

The motto over the entrance to their headquarters reads: "God Is with Us!"

Do you know the Christ who can make this difference? No matter how desperate your situation may be—or that of the world around you, listen to him: "In the world there is tribulation; but be of good cheer; I have overcome the world." There is a story about someone asking the devil what he missed most about being banished from heaven. He replied, "The bugles in the morning!" God's bugles are sounding for us each morning of our lives.

Forgive, Lord, for the ease with which we give up and buckle in to difficult circumstances. Challenge us to respond with the victory of your life. Amen.

The Gift of Healing

He went round the whole of Galilee, teaching in the synagogues, preaching the gospel of the Kingdom, and curing whatever illness or infirmity there was among the people.

MATTHEW 4:23

The Bible lists an amazing array of diseases: boils, epilepsy, fever, insanity, leprosy, loss of appetite, palsy, ague, issue of blood, itch, sunstroke, ulcers. Of Jesus, it is said that he healed all who came to him. In Matthew 10:1 we read, "Then he called his twelve disciples to him and gave them authority to cast out unclean spirits and to cure every kind of ailment and disease." The church in today's world needs to reclaim this authority. Our faith has become so watered down that very few of us really believe in God's power to cure all manner of disease.

Certainly I want to acknowledge the miraculous power of modern medicine. I believe God gives the knowledge to our medical men to discover amazing antibiotics and healing medicines; to be able to skillfully use the knife to remove or remedy damaged areas of the body. Countless miracles take place daily in our hospitals.

But I believe, also, that God in his creative, almighty power can produce healing beyond the comprehension of the finest doctors. And I've heard some of them acknowledge such cases with the words, "It's a miracle."

Dedicated persons who are trying to recover for the church this gift of God stress a point we should keep in mind. We pray for total healing of the person: body, mind, and spirit. The ultimate goal is a closer relationship with God. Emily Gardiner Neal, a leader of The Order of St. Luke, says, "From the early days of my research in the healing ministry, I have been most impressed not by the healings of the body but by the consecrated lives I have observed."

Yet she recounts in a single healing mission such amazing healings as to make one gasp. A blind woman with glaucoma, led to the altar by a friend, received the laying on of hands, then cried out, "I can see! I can see!"

An elderly man, deaf for 18 years, heard "Jesus" as the first word spoken in the prayer. A woman with an open lesion the size of a half dollar on her cheekbone, tugged at Mrs. Neal's skirt and said, "Look, it's a miracle! I've been healed!"

Should we not face the fact that not daring to claim God's promises or accept his gifts, we have rejected him as Lord?

We need to get the focus straight! Bishop John Wright, in addressing a group of physicians, has so well said, "We pray for miracles; we even have seen miracles; but the seeking of miracles is not the purpose of our prayer. The purpose is reconciliation with God."

God has given to some the special gift of healing. He gives to each of us a measure of it as in *faith* we acknowledge him and believe nothing is too hard for him. There is miraculous healing to be had in prayer, and that avenue is open for everyone.

My faith has been so small, Lord, At the very words of cancer or heart trouble, I cringe! Your almighty power and your amazing love for us are almost lost in my mind and life. Increase my faith. Give me courage to claim your promises, that the results might draw people to acknowledge you and glorify you. Amen.

Necessity or Luxury?

Others again receive the seed among thistles; they hear the word, and worldly cares and the false glamor of wealth and all kinds of evil desire come in and choke the word, and it proves barren. MARK 4:18-19

The parable from which these verses are taken has a beautiful setting. The crowd that followed Jesus to the lakeside was so large that he had to get into a boat on the lake, and as the gospel writer records, "There he sat, with the whole crowd on the beach right down to the water's edge!" Many in that crowd earned their livelihood by sowing and reaping so they could well envision the parable.

What were the worldly cares and false glamor of wealth in that day, we wonder. Surely according to our standards, we would have considered them minimal. No indoor plumbing, no car (very few had even a donkey), no TV, no boat, no snowmobile. In his book, *Becomers*, Keith Miller suggests that in the Middle Ages life was crude, dirty, short, and miserable. And so the church concentrated on the beauty and glory of heaven. Christians today are often accused of living for the prospect of "pie in the sky, by and by." If material possessions and the comforts of life were the ultimate, what more could heaven offer than what we enjoy here and now? But has the possessing of many things made our lives richer? Has the piling up of things brought more of the joy of living and loving?

We need to take inventory of our possessions. Which are necessities? which luxuries? Next time we go shopping we would do well to pause and hear the Lord say, "Do we really need that?" Facetiously I have said, "The joy of window shopping is that you see all the things you can get along without."

Elton Trueblood once told us that he carries a little cross in his coin purse. When he fingers the coins for a purchase, inevitably he will feel the cross which reminds him to ask himself, "Do I really need it?"

The causes of Christ in his love for humanity wouldn't go begging if more of us would practice this.

Scripture says, "Worldly cares and the false glamor of wealth choke the word." Here is the tragedy. Are we exchanging grain, grain that produces flour that makes bread, for thistles?

Take inventory!

My home is filled with things I don't really need, Lord, and yet I go out and buy more. I haven't even cupboard space enough. Help me not to get caught up in the rash of compulsive buying. Weed out the thistles that would choke out the Word! Amen.

Running Away

But Jonah set out for Tarshish to escape from the Lord.   JONAH 1:3

To get the whole picture of man running away from God, read the entire book of Jonah. The four brief chapters require no more than ten minutes. We need to take a look at this running away business because most of us have tried it sometime in our lives in one way or another. I don't mean necessarily in the body; not many have packed a bag and left home. But how often mentally and spiritually have we run away? Why do so many young people try it, why do they try to "get lost?"

Karen, 14, gives lack of communication and understanding as her reason. Jack's mother thinks it's affluence. A clinical psychologist says it's the human trait of escapism, blaming someone else. Could it be because our homes are not what they might be?

We need to take inventory of ourselves, too. From what do I run away? Why do I run away?

I run away from seeing myself as God sees me when the moments of truth come. It isn't easy to be honest at those points. What are my motives for participation in church activities? Am I impelled by "everybody's doing it?" Is the motivation a rugged sense of duty, or what will happen to me if I don't? Is it because I want people to think well of me that I want to give the "Christian" image?

I run away from admitting I was wrong and saying, "Forgive me." And even when I do say it, I want a similar response from the recipient of my apology.

We chuckle about it now, but it wasn't so funny at the time. My husband was taking me to the Chicago airport to catch a plane for Colorado where I was participating in a retreat. The Kennedy Expressway on which we traveled was a moving parking lot. I was beside myself for fear of missing the plane, so I became the driver's helper. "Turn this way!" "Look out, there's a truck." Finally my ordinarily patient husband turned to me and said, "I'll drive this car!" Was I ever hurt!

I looked out the window until the Holy Spirit finally got through enough for me to turn to Clarence and say, "Forgive me. I didn't mean to make it hard." His response made me gulp! He said, "I accept your apology!"

Maybe one of the things we run away from most is involvement. Real, daily, nitty-gritty involvement. Putting our lives on the line.

Jonah wanted to spurn the people of Nineveh, even though God had commanded him to go there. He took instead a ship to the farthest out part of the then known world. And en route he encountered a frightful storm. He had literally to lose his life to find it again. And when God offered his mercy in response to Ninevites' turning to him in repentance, Jonah sat down in a blue funk and pouted.

From what are you running away?

You are everywhere, Lord! How can we run away from you? Turn us about to face you and to learn what you have for us to do. Do it today, Lord, in these quiet moments. Amen.

Who Is Our Neighbor?

And Jesus concluded, "In your opinion, which one of these three acted like a fellow-man toward the man attacked by the robbers?" The teacher of the Law answered, "The one who was kind to him." Jesus replied, "You go, then, and do the same."

LUKE 10:36-37 (TEV)

A 25-year-old man shot himself after leaving a note saying his car stalled in frigid weather and no motorists would stop to help him. "I have been waiting 11 hours for someone to stop," said the note found next to his body. "I can't stand the cold any longer and they just keep passing by."

Newspapers often report stories of failure to respond to human need. The excuse is, "We don't want to be involved." Isn't the haunting memory that you might have saved a person a greater curse? Is it enough to avoid danger just to save our physical lives? Jesus gave quite another directive: "If anyone wants to come with me, he must forget himself, carry his cross, and follow me. For whoever wants to save his own life will lose it, but whoever loses his life for my sake will find it" (Matthew 16:24-25 TEV).

Most of us live a lukewarm, dull, unexciting life because we make so little commitment to others. In recent years the younger generation has shown far more courage in putting their lives on the line than we have. We are so protective of ourselves; we don't want to be disturbed.

While there is yet time, God is calling us. We will find fulfillment as we dare to love and respond. Maybe the calls for help aren't as dramatic as the ones in news stories. Maybe some lonely neighbor needs to know you care. Some aged person longs for love. Someone in your own family needs a listening ear. Some humanitarian cause to which you have turned a deaf ear needs you now. It's good to be needed. It's the purpose for living.

Of this I am sure. If you pray for God to make you aware of what his plans are for you today, he will do it. As you study his Word, and are quiet before him, he will put into your mind those you should be remembering. But take time to listen to him. And then be willing to obey!

A rich man was complaining, "Everybody criticizes me. How can they do that when they know I've left everything to charity when I die?"

A friend answered him by telling him a story about a pig and a cow. The pig was lamenting to the cow about how unpopular he was. "People are always talking about your gentleness and kind eyes. Sure, you give milk and cream. But I give much more. I give bacon and ham, and bristles. Why they even pickle my feet. Still nobody loves me. Why is this?"

The cow thought a moment and then said, "Well, maybe it's because I give while I'm still living."

What is your response to calls for help?

Lord, help me to recognize my neighbor in every call for help. You know that I can't answer them all, Lord, but don't let me use that as an excuse for answering none. Guide me day by day to be about your errands of love. Amen.

For Such
a Time

Teach us to order our days rightly,
that we may enter the gate of wis-
dom.   PSALM 90:12

After reading your newspaper you may have paused to consider the times in which we live. You could say, "Horrible! These are terrible times!" You could list the stories of murder and war, of hatred and violence, lust and licentiousness.

You could also remember the marvels of communication, of the speed of air transportation, of the "one world" we know through telestar. Scientists tell us that these are but a glimpse of what will still be. It is a dangerous time to be alive, depending on where your focus is.

When Apollo XIII ran into trouble 205,000 miles from earth, scientists working with computers figured out the correct return flight in just 84 minutes. Working with paper and pencil in the pre-computer age, it would have taken one man 1,040,256 years. We are told that whole wars could be fought with computers.

The laser beam is revolutionizing science. Metals can be welded by it, and machine guns and rockets fired by it. The laser can treat growths in inaccessible parts of the human body. It can rejoin detached retinas to the eye.

These things could turn this world into a paradise or a holocaust. It depends on how they are used. What then is the determining factor?

You and I are the ones who can make the difference! God is calling us in these exciting times to get our lives into focus, to really put him at the center, to redeem the time in loving concern for others. Pope John said it well: "It would be scarcely necessary to expound doctrines if our lives were radiant enough. If we behaved like Christians there would be no pagans. What is important is to love one another. . . ." Someone else has said, "You can tell how great your God is by your concept of other people." And George Muller's definition of a Christian is very succinct and real. "A Christian is a mind through which Christ thinks; a heart through which Christ loves; a voice through which Christ speaks; a hand through which Christ helps!"

Does this describe you? Are we challenged to get into focus, not only as individuals, but corporately, as a church, a community? We need to be joining hands in the causes of mankind. What are our priorities? Is it the concern over increased taxes or is it deep-level concern over where the money is spent? Are we in our affluence really willing to identify with the poor and reflect Christ's concern for them?

Martin Niemoller tells of the word his father passed on to him: "Son, go to the last day of your life and let it your keeper be." From this telling perspective, what would your focus be?

Brother Andrew tells of a worshiping congregation in an iron curtain country. They lived with the uncertainty of secret police coming through the door. Then one night it happened. There was a loud banging on the door, and when it was opened, there stood a huge gendarme with a machine gun in his hand. He bellowed forth, "Whoever is afraid to die for Christ had better get out now!"

At first there was stunned silence, then one by one several left. But there were those who remained.

The intruder then proceeded to lock the door and strode to the front. Throwing down his machine gun he lifted up his arms and said, "I am one of you. But I didn't dare admit it before those who were afraid to die for Christ!"

The question for us this day: Are we daring to *live* for him?

Life can never be dull again,
When once you've thrown the win-
dow open wide,
And seen the great world that lies
outside,
And said to yourself this wondrous
thing:
I'm wanted for the business of the
King!

Get me in focus, Lord. Help me to live for you! Amen.

Varieties
of Gifts

*There are varieties of gifts, but the
same Spirit. . . .
One man, through the Spirit has the
gift of wise speech. . . . another by
the same Spirit is granted faith; . . .
another by the same spirit, gifts of
healing; . . . yet another has the gift
of ecstatic utterance of different kinds.
. . .*   1 CORINTHIANS 12:4, 8-10

The cliché, "variety is the spice of
life," might well be taken out of its
mothballs and aired again. What a witness to the amazing
wonder of God the Creator is the variety of nature. Not only
are there countless species of things, but within each species
there are infinite differences. No two alikes: snowflakes, leaves,
blades of grass—and greatest wonder of all, human beings.

There are common denominators of course, and often
only under microscopic examination can the differences be
discerned. But this fact remains: there is no one exactly like
you.

I have two overwhelming reactions to this stupendous
thought. First of all, I want to bow in worshiping the magnitude of such a God, the creator. How puny our finite minds
are in the light of infinite knowledge and wisdom! All the
amazing discoveries and inventions witness to what has always been in God's creation, and how little we have known.
Who can say what is to come?

The second reaction hits right home .There is no one

just like me. So God has a special purpose for me—whatever my gifts—obvious or hidden. In the circle in which I live and work, he expects me to be a climate-changer. How often I have envied someone with the gift of a beautiful voice and thought, "If I had a voice like that, how I'd use it to sing praise to God." And all the while, I well may be failing to use my speaking voice to share his love.

God is asking you to take honest inventory of his gifts to you! Thank him for them, and use them to his glory in finding loving ways to serve your fellowmen.

I was sitting in a beauty parlor in Aviano, Italy, some years ago and overhead two women waiting to be served. The first woman was telling of some of the things she had been making. Then in something of a whine the second woman said, "You're so talented! You can do just about everything. I have no talent; there isn't anything I can do."

Perhaps it was rude for me to interrupt, but I believe the Spirit nudged for I said, "Pardon me, but that isn't true. You have the greatest gift of all! You can love."

Lord, I have often excused myself from being used by you. As I have looked at others with their gifts and found mine seemingly inadequate, I've pulled into a shell of stony inactivity. Forgive me, and help me to take honest inventory. And by the enabling of your Spirit, help me manage well those endowments you have given me. Amen.

Is It a Good Buy?

You fool! This very night you will have to give up your life; then who will get all these things you have kept for yourself?   LUKE 12:21 (TEV)

One would do well to read the entire parable with which Jesus concludes this decisive question. And we need to ponder the "bargains" that we have made.

A cartoon shows a woman with a shopping cart pausing before a sign: "Special Offer! 20% off All 30% Increases!"

Of course the point is the irony of inflation, but it also suggests how gullible we can be and how tawdry our values are. The Old Testament prophet cries out, "Why do you spend money for that which is not bread; and your labor for that which does not satisfy?"

Isn't part of the problem in America that we want more and more? Think of what we look like to the rest of the world. Think of what your living looks like to those who live in the slums.

We have often heard our daughter say, "Less is more!"

A story about skylarks says that grandfather skylark takes the grandson high into the air to help train him. All the while the elder tells the younger about the proud history of the larks, how they fly higher and soar more gracefully than any other bird. This little bird had only half an ear cocked to his grandfather's voice. His eyes were on a little man in the field below who was carrying an enticing sign,

"Worms for sale; worms for skylark feathers." While his grandfather was absorbed in his rhetoric, the little bird swooped down to the man and asked how much. The reply was, "One worm for two skylark feathers." Who would miss two feathers? So the little bird made the transaction and was back at the grandfather's side. This was repeated each of the following days, until Saturday came. Then there was a bargain; five worms for ten skylark feathers.

The temptation to such a feast was too great for the little winged one, and he made the bargain. But when the ten feathers were plucked, he couldn't lift himself off the ground. He had sold his wings for worms.

"Why do you spend money for that which is not bread?"

When I think of the distorted values that often possess me, Lord, I am ashamed. I am haunted by my time values as well as my possession values. Help me to know that life has no bargains, that there is no short cut to following you. Amen.

Let's Talk
It Over

*Hear, O Israel, the Lord is our God,
one Lord, and you must love your
God with all your heart and soul and
strength. These commandments
which I give you this day are to be
kept in your heart; you shall repeat
them to your sons, and speak of them
indoors and out of doors, when you
lie down and when you rise.*

DEUTERONOMY 6:4-7

An article in a youth magazine was
titled, "When was the last time you
had a heart to heart talk with your Dad?" A similar question
applies to us all. "When did you last have a heart to heart
talk with anybody?"

We live most of our lives on the surface and rarely
get beyond the outer crust. Think through the average conversation. How much does it deal with life at its gut level?
Because our young people have known so little communication in depth with their parents, the so-called generation
gap has developed. Because employer and employee have
fenced with each other on the surface, labor and manage-
ment are constantly at loggerheads. Because husbands and
wives so rarely find time to sound each other's depths and
needs there are broken homes and divorces. Because neighbors
know so little about each other's needs, there is misjudgment,
antagonism, and breach.

The words of Deuteronomy suggest that the things of

113

the spirit should be shared in our homes, in our neighborhood, wherever we are!

What makes for a heart to heart talk?

First, there must be honesty. The more we talk in circles and evade, the greater our misunderstanding and foggy relations. It isn't easy many times to come to the heart of the matter. It is like a surgeon's knife. But this is how cancerous growths can be removed and wounds cleansed and healed.

And we must take time. A Christian psychiatrist told of learning to communicate with his patients. He found that often he had to sit quietly and listen in silence for some time before the door opened. He said it was like sitting at a door with just a tiny crack open, watching for a mouse. As you watched you might see the little whiskers emerging, then a pink nose. . . . But if you moved your toe, whisk—back into the hole would go the timid, frightened creature.

We need the wisdom of God to know when to barge in and when to sit quietly and wait. The important thing is that we make the effort to communicate.

There must be honesty, we must take time; and we need to communicate in love. It is all too easy to foist our opinions on others. It is hard to give a sympathetic ear to what they are needing to share.

Do we as Christians communicate to others what God is like? Do we take time to understand their viewpoints.?

Think of the members of your household, your office, your schoolroom, your neighborhood. When have you had a heart to heart talk? There are lonely, heart-hungry people all about us.

Lord, I confess that much of my living is on the surface. Please give me your love so I can be more sensitive to the needs of others! Amen.

Growing Old

You shall rise in the presence of grey hairs, give honor to the aged, and fear your God.   LEVITICUS 19:32

Do not cast me off when old age comes, nor forsake me when my strength fails.   PSALM 71:9

Listen to me, house of Jacob and all the remnant of the house of Israel, a load on me from your birth, carried by me from the womb: till you grow old I am He, and when white hairs come, I will carry you still; I have made you and I will bear the burden, I will carry you and bring you to safety.   ISAIAH 46:3-4

With the span of life lengthening because of new medical discoveries, we have more people in the upper bracket of years than ever before. The inevitability of age like the certainty of death is something we each should face even when we are young. That amazing passage from Ecclesiastes 12 speaks to it: "Remember your Creator in the days of your youth, before the time of trouble comes and the years draw near when you will say, 'I see no purpose in them.'"

Then follows a matchless poetic description of what happens to our bodies: "When the guardians of the house tremble, and the strong men stoop . . . and those who look through the windows look no longer, . . . when the noises of the mill is low, when the chirping of sparrows grows faint . . . when men are afraid of a steep place and the street is full of terrors. . . . Remember him before the silver cord is snapped and the golden bowl broken. . . ."

What a description of failing limbs, of dimming eyesight, of diminishing bearing, of disintegrating teeth, of bodily decay!

Two basic thoughts come to me as I face the inevitability of years and their accompanying decline of bodily powers.

First, as the writer of Ecclesiastes says, we should prepare for growing old in our youth. In his helpful book. *On Growing Old,* Paul Tournier proposes that we each should have two occupations, so that when we are retired we can pick up the second one. For most of us there have been many things we've never had time to do because we've been so busy earning a living. Retirement may be a time when some of these dreams come alive. In her book, *Don't Put on Your Slippers Yet,* Mrs. Anderson gives several case histories of people who have found a whole new dimension after retirement.

But the most important thing is that when you are young you learn to know the joy of God's presence in your life, and the growing and expanding joy of a daily walk with him. Claim for yourself his promise: "I will never leave you nor forsake you!" Maybe that was the basic secret of the old woman who in answer to the question, "How are you?" always replied, "I'm so happy." What a contrast to those who sit around pitying themselves!

A beautiful grace to retain with the advancing years is a sense of humor. We know some delightful people in their eighties who stimulate laughter and joy with a quick turn of phrase like the fellow Mrs. Anna Mau tells about in her book, *Who's Afraid of Birthdays?* He was asked, "How does it feel to be ninety?" To which he replied, "I don't know. I've never been there before."

This little quatrain makes a good prayer for each of us:

> God give me sympathy and sense,
> And help me keep my courage
> high!
> God give me calm and confidence,
> And please, a twinkle in my eye.

Yes, we need to prepare for growing old.

But the second thing that comes to mind is this: what are we who are able, doing to alleviate the loneliness and destitution of old folks in our community? In Chicago my husband buried a woman who had been dead for four days in her apartment. No one bothered to check on her.

The person to person approach can mean so much! If everyone could know that some human being cares, not just at Christmas and Easter, but daily!

I love what a group of young people do in a city on the west coast. In a house to house canvas they learned which folks were housebound in their community. On their way home from school, each would go past the place assigned to him. In a personal visit the arrangement had been made, that if the couple or person needed anything, there was a sign in the window. This might mean grocery shopping or running other errands. Otherwise the sign up would be okay. If no sign was up, the youth would knock at the door.

Not long ago, neighbors broke in to an aged woman's apartment because they were concerned about her welfare. They had seen no sign of her for several days. But it was too late! She had been dead many hours. On her bedside table they found her diary. Fingering through it, they read the trivia she had recorded day by day. Then there were the last three pages. On each was scrawled the same three words: "No one called!"

Is there some one today who will be writing that because you haven't cared enough?

It is a two-way street here: a blessing given, means a blessing received. Meaning in life and joy in being little Christs in shoe leather makes for a deep-down satisfaction and purposeful living.

We attend so many meetings! Maybe we could eliminate some of these and spend those hours being Christ's hands and feet and heart to forgotten old people.

Thank you, loving Lord that you have promised to be with us even to old age. Thank you that our eternal soul knows no age. Thank you for all who care! Amen.

Riches in Heaven

Jesus said to him, "If you wish to go the whole way, go, sell your possessions, and give to the poor, and then you will have riches in heaven; and come, follow me."

MATTHEW 19:21

A rich young ruler came to Jesus one day and told him that he had kept all the commandments and wanted to know where he fell short. Jesus' reply must have surprised him. How do we react? Is the "if" in what Jesus says the key to our reactions? Do we really want to go the "whole way?"

How do we react to the pictures of Ethiopian children dying of hunger? What is our response to the orphans in Vietnam, and Korea, born of American fathers and Asian mothers? What are we doing to become part of God's answer?

In the first instance we need to react individually. What new thing can we get along without to share more generously with someone in need? Those who have had this experience agree that there is no greater joy than being used of God in this way.

Our church in the inner city is able to sponsor an emergency relief program because one man and his wife (not members) decided they wanted to share God's blessings with the poor. And so they give enough for both staff and resource. Their witness is "We have never done anything that has given us such great joy!"

As Christians we also need to respond collectively. We need to be a part of our democratic process with power to work for programs for the poor, the disenfranchised, the dispossessed. We need as a church to re-order our values. Do we need more buildings to provide greater comfort for ourselves? Or do we need concern for people outside of our own membership, as well as in it?

We need as a nation to consider our budget and its priorities. How much do we allow for false self-protection? How much for human concern?

What value do we place on a child's education? How concerned are we about child development centers, for children who haven't the opportunities ours do?

As individuals, as churches, as a nation we need to take inventory of our budgets.

The "if" in Jesus' statement to the rich young ruler is the key. We need to be honest. "If you wish to go the whole way. . . ."

Then the cry of every needy child, the agony of the oppressed, will find a response in our hearts.

Jesus, we read in your Word, that just before this rich man came to you, children were brought to you and the disciples tried to send them away. But you took them in your arms and blessed them. Give us grace to be your arms, Lord, to needy people at home and around the world. Amen.

Who's Afraid of Death?

For he (Jesus Christ) has broken the power of death and brought life and immortality to light through the Gospel.
2 TIMOTHY 1:10

For I am convinced that there is nothing in death or life, in the realm of spirits or superhuman powers, in the world as it is or the world as it shall be, in the forces of the universe, in heights or depths—nothing in all creation that can separate us from the love of God in Christ Jesus our Lord.

ROMANS 8:38-39

Death is the most inevitable experience of all life. It is completely inclusive, without concern for status or accomplishment. Death knows no discrimination. It is a fact every living soul must face. Why then do we avoid speaking about it? Could it be that we need to take a look at the reality of our Christian faith?

The enigma of accidents, so familiar in auto and airline crashes today, was also present in the days Jesus walked on earth. Once he spoke of an occasion when a water tower fell and killed several local people. He was asked the question, "Were those so much more wicked than others that this should have happened to them?" His only answer to the listening people was, "Repent! Be ready whatever befalls you!" The implication is that no one knows when death will tap us on the shoulder. Be always ready!

In his book, *The Bridge of San Luis Rey*, Thornton Wilder relates how a swinging bridge over a deep chasm suddenly broke carrying the people who chanced to be on it to their death. He develops the life story of each one and concludes that this was the appropriate time for death to visit them. Would we say the same of 100 who crash to death on an airliner today?

We need to take a better look at what we mean by living! Surely it isn't how *many* years we live, but how deeply we live that makes the difference.

Pastor Clifford Boreen left this world in his early thirties. Yet those last months of his life when he was completely blind and immobilized with arthritis were fruitful enough to have the value of a whole lifetime. At Bethesda Hospital an orderly would wheel his bed into the hall on Sunday morning so he could preach to the nurses. Many of them gave testimony that those were the most memorable sermons they ever heard.

I remember reading poetry to him one Saturday night, and how he asked me to repeat the lines of this verse:

> A crystal mirror, I.
> Fate flung me, (how prosaic) in the
> dust.
> Now shattered here I lie.
> Lord, help me to try to be
> A rare mosaic in the dust.

Clifford planned every detail of his own memorial service, from the scriptures and prayers to the witness of his very dear friend, Glen Clarke, to the text of my husband's message, and all of it witnessed to his unshakable faith in the resurrected and living Christ as his personal Savior.

Dr. Howard Olson a seminary teacher in Tanzania, told an amazing story in one of his Christmas letters. He told of how the list of Christian martyrs was growing under the cruel regime of the Tutsi government in Burundi, Africa. A minority group rules a majority, and can only maintain this power by generating hatred. Thousands of innocent people are killed. The Christians refuse to be a party to this corroding hatred. One of the pastors named Yona was very outspoken in his desire to effect reconciliation. A missionary warned him on one day that his very life was at stake, and that he should flee. "How can I leave them?" he responded. "They need a pastor!"

In the middle of that very night the police came and took him by force. They put him in a Landrover with two other passengers and drove to a river four miles from his home. They asked him, "Do you have anything to say before we shoot you?" He replied calmly, "Whether you kill me or not is up to you. Even if you kill me I refuse to hate you." Then he walked toward the river singing in his own language, "There is a happy land far far away." While his song was still in the air, they shot him. Then they turned to the third man and said, "We have the two we want. You can go!" He had not been a Christian, but when he saw this pastor's love in the face of death he was converted right there on the spot. He was convinced that the Christian faith must surely be true if it can do this to a man staring death in the face.

In one of their songs the young people of today tell us what to do: "Put Your Hand in the Hand of the Man from Galilee." Then we can say with the Apostle Paul, "O death, where is thy sting? O grave, where is thy victory?" And the motto of our life can be the one that dominated Jan's memorial service, "Whether I live, or whether I die, I am the Lord's!" Jesus' life, death, and resurrection make all the difference!

In his book, *Ideas Have Legs,* Peter Howard quotes an

old farmer's saying, "Live as though you would die tonight; farm as though you would live forever!"

Thank you, Lord, that we can sing, "Thou hast made death glorious and triumphant!" Amen.

What's Your Dream?

Thereafter the day shall come when I will pour out my spirit on all mankind; your sons and your daughters shall prophesy, your old men shall dream dreams and your young men see visions; I will pour out my spirit in those days even upon slaves and slave-girls. I will show portents in the sky and on earth, blood and fire and columns of smoke; the sun shall be turned into darkness and the moon into blood before the great and terrible day of the Lord comes. Then everyone who invokes the Lord by name shall be saved. JOEL 2:28-32

At the very mention of the word "dream" countless biblical instances come to mind. There were the many dreams of the various kings interpreted by the prophets; there were the dreams of Pharaoh, whose interpretation made Joseph so famous and opened for him his prison door. It was a dream that started Samuel on his prophetic career. In a vision Mary learned that she was to be the mother of our Lord; and in a dream Joseph learned he should not put Mary away. Through a dream Mary and Joseph were directed to flee to Egypt to escape Herod's venom. The vision of our Lord appearing to Saul

125

(later Paul) was the one that changed the whole course of his life!

Through the unfolding years of history, dreams and visions have inspired persons to loftier goals and progress. Sometimes the dreams are of personal attainments and power! These result in destruction! But when a dream has its source in God, and he enables the dreamer to pursue it to fulfillment, blessings will follow.

Woodrow Wilson's dream of a world without war, a world negotiating at a table rather than fighting with arms seems to have come to ashes. Yet some have the faith to believe that out of the ashes men might live together in a warless world!

Martin Luther King had a dream that cost him his life. But the dream of equal opportunity for all, of people being accepted as people regardless of race, possessions, or anything else, still lives in the hearts of his followers. He had a vision of the world according to God' plan for justice. Was that what prompted his last request? We are told that for the rally to be held the very evening of his death he had asked that they sing, "Precious Lord, take my hand!"

For a worthy dream to be fulfilled, how tightly we need to grip the hand of our Lord!

What are your personal dreams, for yourself, for your loved ones? I chuckle when I think of my recurrent dream. It always involves my losing my purse, with the concomitant agony that follows. What a joy to awaken and find it was only a dream! It isn't because of the little money in the purse. It's the loss of my glasses, my credit cards, my keys, and sundry other things. I've often wondered how dream-solvers would interpret that recurrence in my nocturnal flights?

There was another dream that often came to me when I was a child. I dreamed that vast sums of money would come right before me and all I had to do was to help myself! As I would reach out to feel it, I would think, "O, this is just a dream!" But no, I could really feel it. Imagine my dis-illusionment in awakening from that one!

Sometimes I have wondered if my dreams are symbolic of the world's worst disease, a self-centered concern over material possessions?

What is *your* dream?

The Lord has a dream for his world. It is that *everyone* should come to know him and his love. He wants to use you as his channel for the fulfillment of that dream. How will you, today, become a part of it? What errands for him will you run? What lonely people will you visit? What words of encouragement will you speak to the downhearted? What prayers will you pray for others? What a glorious chal-lenge, to be used of God to fulfill his dream of inclusive love.

These words by Benjamin E. Mays express it well:

"Approximately nineteen hundred years ago, a Jew of Palestine hung on a cross, between two thieves, because he dreamed a dream—that all men are sons of God, and when we hurt man we hurt God. Some blessed day a stupid world will rise to the divinity of God and acknowledge Jesus as Lord. Then the nations of the earth will know that their armies and navies, battleships and machine guns, airplanes and submarines will never bring peace to a suffering world. And that the acquisition of political, material, and commercial powers are not permanent possessions but are as the vapors of night! They fade and die in the morning of reality. 'What shall I do then with Jesus which is called Christ?' The only answer is: Accept him, in our hearts, in our wills, and in our souls."

The prophet Micah had a dream about the time when swords would be beaten into mattocks and spears into prun-ing hooks and when each man would dwell in peace under his own vine.

The apostle Paul proclaimed the hope that at the name of Jesus every knee should bow and every tongue confess that "Jesus is Lord!"

Is he the Lord of your heart? Then you will dare to

show his colors and offer yourself boldly to be used to make God's dream come true!

Please, Lord, help me to dream your dream of love and peace and justice for all. So infect me with your infection until I rub it off on all I come in contact with. Today make me an instrument of your peace! Amen.